WHY DO ROLLER COASTERS MAKE YOU PUKE?

Over 150
Curious Questions & Intriguing Answers

Andrew Thompson

Ulysses Press

Published in the United States by
Ulysses Press
P.O. Box 3440
Berkeley, CA 94703
www.ulyssespress.com

Printed in the United States by Kingery Printing
10 9 8 7 6 5 4 3

ISBN 978-1-61243-714-9
Library of Congress Control Number 2017938182

Acquisitions Editor: Bridget Thoreson
Managing Editor: Claire Chun
Editor: Shayna Keyles
Proofreader: Renee Rutledge
Front cover design: what!design @ whatweb.com
Cover photos from Shutterstock.com: chair, toad, vulture © Hein Nouwens;
    mouse © lynea; cucumber © Epine; apples © DiViArt; elephant © andrey
    oleynik; watermelon © Sketch Master; pirate © VectorPot; airplane ©
    blue67sign; zebra © mamita; insect © KUCO; goldfish © Vangert; beer ©
    Boule; plant © Ruslan Semichev; photo © IgorGolovniov; cat © Sinelev
Interior photos: see page 211

Distributed by Publishers Group West

To Lucy

⇨ Contents

⇨ Can a Cockroach Survive a Nuclear Bomb?

Cockroaches are resilient creatures that have lived on earth for 300 million years, predating the dinosaurs by 150 million years. After atomic bombs were dropped on Hiroshima and Nagasaki in 1945, reports later emerged that the only survivors in the cities were cockroaches, whose populations seemed largely unaffected. This led many

to believe that roaches can survive nuclear bombs. So, can they, or is this just another urban myth?

To test this theory, various scientific teams have conducted experiments on cockroaches over the last 60 years, exposing them to the radioactive metal cobalt-60, a synthetic substance produced artificially in nuclear reactors. After an exposure of 1,000 radon units (rads), which was the level of radiation detected about 15 miles from Hiroshima directly after the bomb was detonated, capable of killing a person in 10 minutes, most cockroaches survived, although their fertility was severely compromised. After exposure to 10,000 rads, the amount of radiation emitted by the Hiroshima bomb, only one in ten cockroaches survived, and at a level of 100,000 rads, no cockroaches lived.

The ability of cockroaches to withstand extreme radiation owes to the simple design of their bodies and their relatively slow cell cycles. Cells are most sensitive to radiation when they're dividing. The cells of a cockroach divide about every two days, and the insects molt only once a week. The cells of humans, on the other hand, are constantly changing and renewing, making us 10 times more susceptible to radiation than cockroaches.

Cockroaches, however, are nuclear lightweights compared with others in the insect world. It takes 64,000 rads to kill the fruit fly, 100,000 rads to kill the flour beetle, and the Habrobracon, a type of parasitic wasp, can withstand an astonishing 180,000 rads.

In short, while cockroaches would not be able to withstand the direct impact of an explosion, some would be able to survive the radiation produced by a blast on the level of the Hiroshima bomb. They wouldn't survive the far more powerful bombs of today, but they're still impressively hardy bugs. This begs the question: Just how strong is the stuff they put in bug spray, anyway?

⇨ Why Does Traffic Jam for No Apparent Reason?

Everyone has experienced the frustration of a "phantom traffic jam." The traffic just seems to stop for no apparent reason, and by the time you're moving freely again, you cannot see what might have caused it—there is no accident, no roadwork, no police interference. So, why do these jams happen?

If there are enough cars on a highway, any minor disruptions to the flow of traffic can trigger a chain reaction. All it takes is for one car to brake unexpectedly. A driver might get too close to the car in front, look at the scenery and lose concentration, change lanes in front of another car, or

slow because of a bump in the road. The driver then brakes slightly, forcing the unsuspecting drivers behind to react with their own brakes so they can stay at a safe distance. A ripple effect occurs and the braking amplifies backward. It's like a shock wave that becomes more pronounced as it works its way back until a traffic jam is produced.

A phantom traffic jam will take longer to dissipate than it takes to develop, and as you drive forward, the effects of the jam move backward. The front of the jam clears, and by the time the cars at the back are moving freely again, the road in front is almost empty and drivers are left wondering what the problem was in the first place.

A 2008 experiment conducted by Professor Yuki Sugiyama, the head of the Mathematical Society of Traffic Flow at Japan's Nagoya University, had 22 cars drive on a circular road. A phantom traffic jam was soon created, the cars piling up in under a minute. The study showed that the solution to the problem is all about speed and spacing. When people drive a little slower and keep a bigger space between themselves and the car in front, the snowballing effect of sudden braking is avoided and fewer traffic jams occur.

⇨ Do People Really Turn Green with Envy?

Generally seen as something negative, envy is an emotion that occurs when a person desires another's superior possessions, achievements, or qualities, or wishes that the other person didn't have them. Thought to be one of the main causes of unhappiness in people, envy is often associated with the color green. But do people actually turn green with envy? How did this idea come about?

The idea of turning green with envy began in ancient Greece. The Greeks believed that various illnesses, along with what they termed "restless emotions," were accompanied by an overproduction of bile, which lent a pallid green color to a person's complexion. In the 7th century, the Greek poet Sappho described a stricken lover as being "green."

This idea persisted through the ages and was eventually brought to the mainstream by Shakespeare, who popularized the concept in two of his works. In his 1603 play *Othello*, he wrote, "Beware my lord of jealously. It is the green-eyed monster which doth mock the meat it feeds on." He made further reference in his 1605 play *The Merchant of Venice*, when he wrote, "How all the other passions fleet to air, as doubtful thoughts and rash-embraced despair and shuddering fear and green-eyed jealousy!"

So while the Greeks actually believed that green-eyed monsters existed, they don't. It was, in fact, Shakespeare who perpetuated the myth of turning green with envy and turned it into the expression that is still used today.

⇨ Are Elephants Really Afraid of Mice?

Known as musophobia, murophobia, or suriphobia, the fear of mice is one of the most common human phobias. And, since the 1941 Disney classic *Dumbo*, the idea that elephants are afraid of mice has long been a staple joke of cartoons. In fact, the Roman philosopher Pliny the Elder wrote in his 77 AD book *Naturalis Historia*, "of all other living creatures, they [elephants] cannot abide a mouse or a rat." But is there any truth to this seemingly implausible suggestion?

Some say that elephants are afraid of mice because they fear the mice will crawl up their trunks, causing irritation, blockage, and breathing difficulties. However, elephant experts say there is no evidence to support this claim, and that in any event, an elephant could easily blow out and eject the mouse.

Whatever the supposed reason, a number of studies have been conducted over the years to determine whether elephants really are afraid. A series of 1939 experiments found that elephants failed to react when a mouse entered their enclosure, except when the mouse scurried over a sheet of paper. This caused some of the elephants to stand up and trumpet, perhaps spooked by the rustling noise. In a 2006 test conducted at the Ringling Brothers circus, a number of white mice were held up at eye level to various elephants. The elephants didn't react at all, and were said to look "bored." But this may have been because the mice were being held, rather than racing around the elephants' feet. In a more recent experiment, mice that were put into an elephant enclosure caused the elephants to stop dead and even back away and walk off in the other direction. However, scientists believe that it's more likely that the elephants were merely surprised by the mice, not afraid of them.

Indeed, animal behaviorists think that given their poor eyesight, elephants can startle easily and are liable to get scared when anything small rushes by without warning. This has been observed, as the sudden movements of cats, small dogs, snakes—and mice—all make elephants nervous.

So rather than being afraid of the mouse itself, the elephant's fear has more to do with the element of surprise caused by the rodent's quick, frantic movements. A fine line, perhaps, and probably enough to keep the idea of elephantine musophobia alive for many years to come.

⇨ Why Do Thunderstorms Set Off Car Alarms?

In violent thunderstorms, it is not uncommon to hear a number of car alarms sounding. This is because thunder produces shock waves that travel through the air to the ground.

Modern car alarm systems use instruments to detect shock, pressure, and motion.

These detectors monitor for vibrations using a microphone or the car stereo speakers to pick up low-frequency sounds.

The shock waves produced from thunder can set off car alarms in one of two ways. They can shake the ground and the car, which sets off the motion sensors, similar to when a person breaking into a car shakes it and sets off the alarm. Or, the shock waves can cause a change in air pressure, which physically moves the speakers. The speakers then produce an electrical signal that triggers the alarm.

⇨ How Do People Hot-Wire Cars?

Hot-wiring a car involves bypassing the ignition interlock and starting the car without a key. In many films, this process is done very quickly by a car thief who fiddles with a few wires under the steering wheel. Some sparks appear, the car starts, and he speeds away. But is it really that easy?

With cars made after about the year 2000, it's not. Starting them requires digital verification from a chip in the car key. These cars also include a steering column lock and other safety mechanisms, so crossing wires together won't work. Perhaps surprisingly, however, hot-wiring will work for most cars made before that time. Here's how it's done.

After the plastic covering around the steering wheel column is removed, various wires will be exposed. There are usually three sets of wires. Typically, the bundles to the left and right operate things such as lights and windshield wipers, so the wires you're after will run straight up the center of the column. These are the ignition wires (usually brown), the starter wires (usually yellow), and the battery wires (almost always red).

Once the wires are located, strip an inch of insulation from the two battery wires and twist them together to provide power for the ignition components. Then connect the ignition wire to the battery wire. This will cause the dash lights and other electrical components to start. Now, here comes the dangerous part. Strip half an inch of insulation from the starter wire, which will be live, and touch it to the end of the connected battery wires. The car will start and you can drive away. The starter wire can be detached at this point. When you want to stop the engine, simply unfasten the ignition wire from the battery wires.

A more permanent method of starting a car is to drill into the ignition key hole. The idea is to destroy the various lock pins. Once this is done, you can insert a screwdriver and turn it like a key, and the car should start.

⇨ Why Does Bacon Smell So Good?

Very few aromas will get a person's mouth watering like the smell of bacon cooking. Even vegetarians have been known to falter under its powers. But what makes it different from other meats?

When bacon is cooked, it undergoes a process called the Maillard reaction. Named after the 20th century French chemist Louis-Camille Maillard, the Maillard reaction is the chemical process responsible for turning food brown and giving it aroma and flavor. When bacon is heated, the molecular structure of its sugars begins to break down and react with the amino acids that are released. This reaction releases about 150 complex aroma compounds, far more than other foods.

The majority of these compounds are hydrocarbons and aldehydes, both of which give off delicious smells. This happens with most meats, but bacon has a secret weapon. When it has been cured with salt or brine, it contains a higher percentage of nitrates, specifically pyridines, than other meats have. When pyridines mix with the hydrocarbons and aldehydes, a volatile combination explodes, and that's what gives bacon its unique smell.

⇨ How Did the Term "Yankee" Originate?

"Yankee," and its contracted form "Yank," are slang terms used to refer to people from the United States. Within the country, the term applies to people from the northeastern states that were once part of the Union in the American Civil War, while outside the United States, it is used informally to refer to any American.

The term Yankee has a number of suggested etymologies. One is that it derives from a British officer who said that the Cherokee word *eankke*, pronounced like Yankee and meaning "coward," was used by the Native Americans to refer to the settlers. This is incorrect; no such word exists in the Cherokee language. Another theory is that it derives from a Native American mispronunciation of *l'anglais*, the French word for

English, as "Yengees." Most linguists reject this origin as false, as well.

The likely origin of the term dates from the 1680s. The Dutch settlers in New Amsterdam (now New York), applied the name "Jan Kees" to their rival Dutch colonial neighbors in Connecticut. This term is thought to be based on the name "Jan Kaas," a disparaging nickname translated as "John Cheese" that the Flemish had used for Dutchmen generally. Pronounced in Dutch as "Yankees," it evolved to include the English-speaking colonists as well, eventually being used for all Americans.

The term became widespread as a result of the song "Yankee Doodle," which was popular with both the American and the British troops during the American War of Independence in the late 1700s.

⇨ Why Do People Have Eyebrows?

As humans evolved, we lost most of the thick hair that once covered our bodies. But why did we keep that little bit over the eyes, and what purpose does it serve? It might amaze you to discover that those innocent strips of hair could well be the reason we are here today.

Eyebrows assisted greatly in the survival of early man. Apart from deflecting debris and shielding the eyes from the sun, they keep moisture from rain or sweat out of our eyes.

The arch shape diverts the moisture to the side of the face, keeping the eyes dry so that our vision remains clear. This would have helped our ancestors find shelter in the rain, and it would have helped them escape predators. Running from an attack would likely produce sweat, and if sweat got in the eyes, it would have caused irritation, impaired vision, and made it more difficult to escape. Given this survival advantage, natural selection would have picked those who had eyebrows.

Some scientists also suggest that eyebrows, combined with eyelashes, served as eyespots, creating the illusion that a person's eyes were open even when they were asleep. Nighttime predators such as big cats are far less likely to attack prey if they think the prey is watching them. This also would have provided a distinct survival advantage to our ancestors.

Another reason eyebrows were retained is that they play a significant psychological role. They are one of our most expressive facial features and are essential for nonverbal communication. The different positions and movements of eyebrows are key to signaling change in mood, such as expressing surprise, happiness, and anger. This was important from an evolutionary perspective, as early man's survival hinged on strong-functioning and close-knit tribes.

Eyebrows are also a very distinctive aspect of human appearance and act as identification cards. They stand out from the forehead and can be clearly seen from a distance. This would have been helpful for early man in distinguishing between friend and enemy on the open plains. In fact, experiments have shown that we can recognize a familiar face more easily when the eyes are blanked out than when the eyebrows are. This was shown in a 2002 study published by students at the Massachusetts Institute of Technology. In 60 percent of all trials, people were able to successfully recognize photos of celebrities with their eyes edited out, compared with a 46 percent success rate when the eyebrows were removed.

⇨ How Are Seedless Watermelons Made?

Seedless watermelons are developed so that they possess no mature seeds. As they are easier and more enjoyable to eat, they are far more commercially valuable. But how are they made, and if there are no seeds in them, how are they sustainable?

Watermelon plants are diploid, meaning they have two sets of chromosomes, just as humans do. Seedless watermelons are triploid, meaning they have three sets of chromosomes. To produce a triploid seedless watermelon, a diploid male is crossed with a tetraploid female (it doesn't

work the other way around). Tetraploids, which have four sets of chromosomes, are produced when a chemical called colchicine is applied to diploid seedlings. Colchicine causes some cells to double and become tetraploids.

The pollen from the male diploid is placed on the female flower of the tetraploid. The resulting seed is that of a triploid seedless watermelon. Once planted, pollination triggers fruit development. However, the triploid watermelons don't produce much pollen, so they must be grown alongside some diploid plants to provide pollen and stimulate the seedless watermelon to produce fruit.

Because of the odd number of chromosomes, seedless watermelon are sterile and do not produce seeds. This means they do not self-propagate and the process described above has to be done anew each time, although it does not involve any genetic modification. It's much like the story of the mule, which is produced by crossing a horse with a donkey—a lot of work resulting in a sterile hybrid.

⇨ Can People Really Wake Up After Years in a Coma?

A coma is a state of unconsciousness where a person fails to respond to any stimuli such as pain or sound. People generally cannot be awakened from a coma and have to come out of it themselves. Most comas only last a few days or weeks, but can people wake up after many years to find themselves living in a completely different world?

How fast a person comes out of a coma depends on its cause and the severity of damage to the brain. Many people who enter a coma after overdosing on drugs or alcohol wake up once the substance has cleared their system. A massive brain injury or brain tumor, however, can lead to a much longer coma. Sometimes these comas are irreversible, but on other occasions, the person does wake up after a long period.

A police officer from Tennessee, named Gary Dockery, was shot in the head in the line of duty in 1988. Twenty percent of his brain was removed during surgery, although it was too risky to remove the bullet. He lay in a coma for over seven years. One day, his family was by his bed arguing about what treatment should be given for an illness he had contracted while unconscious. During the discussion, he suddenly woke up and started talking.

There are a number of examples like that one, but the story of Terry Wallis is quite extraordinary. In 1984, Terry was involved in a car crash in Arkansas that left him in a coma. He was just a teenager at the time, and had a wife and a six-week-old daughter. He lay in a coma for 19 years before suddenly waking up. The first thing he said upon awakening was "Mom," when he saw his mother sitting there. He then said "Pepsi," and then "milk," before gradually talking in full sentences. The memories of his conscious life were good, but the world as he knew it had completely changed. He had missed the computer and Internet boom, wars in the Middle East, and a couple of US presidents. His daughter had become an adult and his wife was middle-aged. Doctors were unsure why Terry came out of his coma, but they believe that his brain rewired itself over time and that once there were enough connections, he just woke up. They also believe that the constant contact with his family over the 19 years probably helped his recovery by keeping his mind active and his memory intact.

⇨ Why Are Mosquitoes More Attracted to Certain People?

Picture the scenario: You're at an outdoor barbecue, you decided to wear shorts, you don't have any insect repellent on, the sun has just set, and though nobody else seems affected, you're being eaten alive by mosquitoes. There is nothing more annoying! In between slapping your legs and clapping the air in frustration, you ponder, "Why am I being singled out?"

Around one in ten people are highly attractive to mosquitoes, and a lot of research has been done to find out why. Mosquitoes use smell to identify their prey, and they can detect human scents from up to 160 feet away.

Mosquitoes are particularly attracted to the carbon dioxide that we exhale. In addition to carbon dioxide, every time we exhale we also release uric acid, octenol, and lactic acid. The specific combination of these chemicals in certain people makes them more attractive to mosquitoes. And it's not just the scent of this unique cocktail that mosquitoes are keen on; it's the quantity, too. Large people tend to exhale more, so they are prime targets, as are pregnant women, who exhale above-average amounts.

Besides this carbon dioxide concoction, mosquitoes like sweat, especially sweat that has combined with bacteria, also known as body odor. Everybody's odor is different and depends on the acids, ammonia, and other compounds emitted with the sweat. Mosquitoes prefer some mixtures to others. They also like heat, so a hot and sweaty person is perfect.

Blood type is the other key determinant of whether you'll be bitten more often. People with different blood types secrete different scents, and mosquitoes have been found to be twice as attracted to people with Type O blood compared to those with Type A blood, while those with Type B blood fall somewhere in between.

And then there's this weird one. A study found that significantly more mosquitoes landed on people after they had been drinking beer, although scientists could not fathom why. And it was only one study. One study isn't conclusive, is it?

In the end, genetics accounts for 85 percent of our susceptibility to mosquito bites, but to minimize your risk of being bitten, here's what to do: Let everybody else do the running around, because their movement will attract mosquitoes, as will the excess carbon dioxide they expel by panting and the acids they exude by sweating. Your best bet is to lean back in a nice, comfortable chair and, after warning everybody else that beer attracts the little cretins, take the risk and drink it all yourself.

⇨ Can Staring at a Solar Eclipse Make You Go Blind?

A solar eclipse is when the moon passes between the sun and the earth and fully or partially blocks the sun. This celestial event is quite rare, so when it does happen, people are often inclined to take a look. And just how much damage can a quick peek do, anyway?

It is difficult to stare at the sun under normal conditions and, if you do, the eye will automatically respond to protect the retina by contracting the pupil.  You will also squint or look away without even thinking. However, during an eclipse, with most of the sun covered and not as bright, it is far easier to stare at it, and the protective reactions of your eye do not occur. But even with 99 percent of the sun's surface blocked by the moon, the visible 1 percent that you can see around the edges is just as intense and strong, so looking at an eclipse would be like looking at the full sun with unprotected eyes.

The sun's radiation that enters the eye during an eclipse can damage the rod and cone cells in the retina. Like brain cells, these cells don't regenerate, and exposure to the sun can leave them severely damaged. Known as solar retinopathy, this condition can result in blindness.

To make matters worse, the retina has no sensitivity to pain, so there is no warning that any injury is occurring. In addition, the effects of retinal damage may not appear for hours, so the victim is left unaware for a while. Looking through an optical device such as binoculars is even more dangerous, and can cause irreversible damage immediately.

In essence, looking at the sun during an eclipse is as dangerous as looking at it normally. Like a quick look at the sun on a bright day, a fleeting glance during an eclipse is unlikely to cause permanent damage. But if you look for 10 minutes or more, there is a good chance of incurring some degree of blindness.

⇨ How Did Bread and Dough Come to Mean Money?

Both "bread" and "dough" have been used as slang words for money for years. But what is the connection between these staple foodstuffs and our hard-earned greenbacks?

The word "bread" was first used as slang for money in ancient Greece, when the food was used as a form of currency. Then, in the 1st century AD, the Roman satirist Juvenal coined the expression "Bread and Circuses" to refer to benefits and entertainment for placating the masses. This was in response to the new Roman Empire providing bread as a form of currency to the populace, as well as gladiatorial contests as a form of amusement. Bread was later used as a form of currency in medieval England.

By the early 18th century, the word was being used to mean "livelihood or subsistence." In Daniel Defoe's landmark novel of 1719, *Robinson Crusoe*, he wrote, "I was under no necessity of seeking my bread." Bread continued to be a traditional everyday necessity of life and had become synonymous with money by the 19th century.

By its association with bread, "dough," too, had come to mean money by the mid-19th century. This term became more widespread in the 1920s, when gangsters in Chicago used the word "sourdough" to refer to counterfeit money, possibly owing to their extortion of the city's bakeries. Conversely, dough, like bread, referred to genuine money.

⇨ Why Are Elderly People Bad Drivers?

Driving is a complicated task that requires the use of a number of senses, as well as advanced motor skills. Drivers need to see and hear clearly, pay close attention to a number of factors, and react quickly to unexpected events.

As people reach old age, it is common for most of these faculties to decline. Eyesight and hearing abilities are reduced, reaction time is much slower, reflexes are diminished, and cognitive functions such as concentration decline. Stiffening joints and weaker muscles can also make it more difficult to turn the head, steer the wheel quickly, or hit the brake suddenly. The peripheral vision of elderly people, an ability essential to safe driving, is also generally narrower than in young people.

Statistics show that older drivers are more likely to get into accidents in various situations, such as by failing to obey traffic signals at intersections, by hitting another car that is merging, or while changing lanes. These types of accidents are usually because of the physical decline of the elderly. Older people also tend to drive a lot slower, which can lead to frustration in other drivers that can cause accidents.

But another surprising factor hinders elderly drivers—their enhanced vision. In a 2011 study conducted by a team of scientists led by University of Rochester Professor Duje Tadin, it was found that old people are better at perceiving background motion. The problem is that this is not a good thing when driving. The middle temporal visual area of the brain, or MT, suppresses background motion so that the more important motions of small objects in the foreground can be better seen. The brain cannot process every bit of visual information, so it must use its limited resources to concentrate on the motions of smaller objects. From an evolutionary perspective, this was important, because focusing on small moving objects like prey or enemies was essential for survival. By placing magnetic coils on the back of the subjects' heads, the researchers discovered that the MT in elderly people was often impaired. This meant they could easily identify the motion of large background objects, such as trees or rivers, but had more difficulty seeing the more important smaller objects that were closer. When driving, these smaller objects are cars, people, and traffic lights.

⇨ Why Do Vultures Circle Above Their Prey?

Vultures are a common sight in the skies above the American and African plains. These scavenging birds of prey are often seen circling in the sky before flying down and eating a meal. This has led people to question why they waste their time circling above, and don't just go straight down and eat. There are a number of reasons for this behavior.

Contrary to popular belief, circling vultures does not necessarily mean there is a dead animal below. They soar on warm, rising thermal wind currents for various reasons—to conserve energy, to gain altitude for long flights, and to search for food.

When they are looking for food, vultures locate it by both sight and smell. By flying high up and circling the ground, they are able to scan a large area for food with their excellent vision. They also have a keen sense of smell, and circling may

indicate that they have detected a carcass and are trying to pinpoint its exact location.

Once the vultures have located food, they will often swoop straight down and eat it. But when they keep circling, it is likely to be for one of the following reasons:

- While vultures usually feed on carrion, they will sometimes kill injured or helpless animals. They are, however, very cautious about approaching a live animal, and may circle to ensure it is really dead or incapacitated and not a threat.
- Vultures will always check for any predators that might be in the area, such as a coyote or lion. To scan the area for dangerous animals, they will circle before descending to their meal.
- Vultures will circle over a kill made by a larger predator, like a lion. Lions won't share their kill and will attack any vultures that venture too close. While they're biding their time and waiting for their chance, they will often remain in the safety of the sky.
- If they see a lot of animal activity below, they will some-times circle around waiting for a predator to make a kill that they might be able to scavenge.

So there are a number of valid reasons for vultures to circle the sky, and besides, maybe they're just having fun.

⇨ What's on the Rags that Villains Use to Make People Pass Out?

A villain sneaks up behind an unsuspecting target, places a rag over their mouth, and almost instantaneously the victim

goes weak at the knees and falls to the ground unconscious—we've all seen it many times in movies. But what's on
the rag, and is this even possible?

The rag is doused with chloroform, a colorless, sweet-
smelling liquid that has been used for its anesthetic properties
for years. It was first used in this way by James Young
Simpson in 1847, when he administered it to two friends for
entertainment purposes. After that, it quickly became a common anesthetic agent.

While it can be used as an anesthetic, the way it is used
in the movies is flawed. A chloroform-soaked rag could
render a victim unconscious, but it would take far longer than
portrayed in fiction. Even with a perfectly measured dose, it
would take at least a few minutes. And even then, a continuous volume of chloroform would need to be administered to
keep the person under.

There are other issues with the rag method, making it
implausible. Chloroform is a highly volatile liquid that loses
concentration very rapidly when it is exposed to oxygen. By
the time the rag is pressed to the victim's face, it is likely that
the chemical would have dissipated and become ineffective.

So what you see in the movies is completely unrealistic,
but let's hope no Hollywood producers read this book. If
they do, it might lead to some pretty boring scenes as we sit
through five minutes of a villain holding a rag to his victim's
face, before sitting there and administering more chloroform
to make sure it works.

⇨ Why Does Your Nose Run in Cold Weather?

Known technically as rhinorrhea, a runny nose in cold weather is caused by two reasons: the body protecting itself, and physics.

Our noses warm and humidify the air we breathe so that it is closer to body temperature as it enters the lungs. To do this, the nasal cavities are coated with liquid mucus. This mucus also helps to prevent bacteria, viruses, and other foreign bodies from entering the body. When the weather is cold and dry, the nose dries out, so the mucous membranes work harder to increase fluid production to protect the sensitive lung tissue. Often, more mucus is produced than is necessary, and this excess drips out of the nose.

The second reason the nose runs in cold weather is based on simple physics. The body heats the air you breathe in, so by the time it is exhaled, the air is warm and moist. When the water vapor in your breath hits the cold and dry air near the nostrils, condensation occurs, and droplets of water are formed near the end of your nose. Then gravity takes over.

A runny nose in cold weather can be reduced by negating the physics—breathe in through your nose and out through your mouth.

⇨ Why Don't Women Have Adam's Apples?

Known as the laryngeal prominence, the Adam's apple is the lump in the human neck caused by the protective thyroid cartilage surrounding the larynx. It is often clearly visible in adult men, but women have one, too. So why can't theirs be seen?

The Adam's apple is more prominent in men because of the meeting point of the two portions of cartilage. In men, the angle is about 90 degrees, which pushes the cartilage forward, whereas in women, the angle is an open arc of about 120 degrees.

The protruding angle of the thyroid cartilage in men is formed during puberty. At that time, as testosterone levels increase, the male larynx, or voice box, develops quickly. This not only deepens the man's voice, but pushes the cartilage outward, making it more visible. A woman's larynx also grows, but not nearly as much. Women also tend to have a higher percentage of body fat than men do, which disguises the Adam's apple.

The Adam's apple is named from the Biblical legend where Eve gave Adam the forbidden fruit, which he ate. According to the tale, a piece of it got stuck in his throat and made a lump. Unfortunately for men, the Adam's apple makes it very noticeable when men swallow, a tell-tale sign that they are lying, so that one piece of fruit has been punishing them ever since.

⇨ Does an Apple a Day Keep the Doctor Away?

Dating from the 1860s, "an apple a day keeps the doctor away" is one of our most recognizable expressions. But is there any medical truth to it?

Numerous studies have been conducted regarding apples and their health properties. The fruit undoubtedly has many benefits, and as a rule, more benefits than most other fruits.

Apples contain pectin, a form of soluble fiber that lowers blood pressure and glucose levels. They also contain boron, which is known to support strong bones and a healthy brain, as well as vitamin C, which boosts immunity and overall health. Studies have shown that eating apples lowers cholesterol, reduces the risk of strokes and diabetes, helps with allergies, and regulates a person's weight.

The peel of the apple provides the most health benefits. It contains phytonutrients, which are antioxidant compounds that fight potential damage from free radicals and significantly reduce the risk of heart disease, asthma, and cancer. In one Chinese clinical trial conducted between 2004 and 2014, apple eaters were shown to have a 40 percent lower chance of cardiovascular disease, a 34 percent lower chance of heart attack, and a 30 percent lower chance of stroke. Another study treated cancer cells with an extract from apple skin.

Cancer cell growth was shown to reduce by between 43 and 57 percent, depending on the type of cancer.

Based on all this, apples are obviously a superfood, but does eating one each day reduce visits to the doctor?

A 2015 study at the University of Michigan found that the people who ate an apple a day had, in fact, visited the doctor fewer times in the previous year. However, these same people were less likely to smoke, tended to be more educated, and were less likely to be from an ethnic minority group. After adjusting for these differences, the researchers concluded that there was no statistical significance regarding apples and doctor visits.

So, an apple a day may not keep the doctor away, but, statistically speaking, it will reduce your chances of contracting major diseases and it will make you live longer. But the downside for kids is that you have to eat the skin for the real health benefits to kick in. Is there a trade-off? Apples act as a toothbrush, cleaning the teeth and killing bacteria, so this might give kids an excuse not to brush. How do you like them apples?

⇨ How Did the Military Term "GI" Originate?

GI is a term currently used to refer to a member of the US armed forces, especially an enlisted soldier, although that's not how it started out.

Though now typically used as an acronym for Government Issue or General Issue, the letters GI originally referred to Galvanized Iron. They were used by the US Army logistics services from 1907 to denote equipment made from galvanized iron, such as metal trash cans, in the inventory and supply records. During World War I, American soldiers then began referring to incoming German artillery shells as "GI cans."

It was also during World War I that GI was interpreted as Government Issue, or General Issue, for the general items and equipment used by soldiers. By the lead-up to World War II, the term had extended to describe the soldiers themselves, who during the war became known as G.I. Joes, regardless of what branch of the armed forces they were in. The term became widespread with the popular 1942 comic strip *G.I. Joe*, created by David Breger, which led to the bestselling action toy produced in the 1960s.

⇨ Why Do Sausages Curl When They're Cooked?

Sausages are generally made by stuffing a pork or beef mixture into a thin, translucent casing. That skin is either a natural pork casing, or more usually, a collagen-based casing designed to act like a natural one.

When a sausage is cooked, the heat causes the collagen skin to contract. Heat is usually applied asymmetrically to the sausage; that is, the side touching the frypan receives far more heat than the top of the sausage does, meaning the skin shrinks at different rates. The sausage curls because the

bottom half of the skin contracts at a faster rate than the top, pulling the ends of the sausage inward.

To stop a sausage from curling, it should be sliced down the center to reduce the pull of the skin. Alternatively, cook it at a lower temperature on an electric stove, which distributes the heat more evenly.

⇨ Why Don't We Eat Horsemeat?

Known as hippophagy, the eating of horsemeat has been practiced across the world for centuries. Still today, many countries consider horse a delicacy, and it is widely available in Asia and parts of Europe, where it outsells mutton and lamb.

Horsemeat is good for you. It's a good source of protein, has a sweet flavor, is tender, contains fewer calories than beef, and has a lot more omega-3 fatty acids than beef. And it's not as if horses are not available or are too expensive. The United States has hundreds of thousands of excess horses that are either abandoned by owners who can't afford them, or are running wild and are damaging their environment.

Yet, since the turn of this century, many laws have been passed throughout the United States effectively banning the slaughter of horses for human consumption.

As a nation, Americans eat a lot of meat, but not horse-meat. Why the uproar?

The reason is thought to stem back to 732 AD, when Pope Gregory III decreed that the ritual consumption of horsemeat was a pagan practice that had to be eliminated. He described hippophagy as a "filthy and abominable custom." Some historians believe that he was trying to preserve horses for warfare, but whatever the reason, the papal ban was effective and dissuaded people from eating horses for centuries.

The residual impact of that decree may have had some influence in the United States over the years, but the real reason Americans don't eat horsemeat is because we love our beasts of burden. Horses have long been a sort of mythological creature in the American national consciousness. From the time they were brought to US shores by the Spanish in the 16th century, they were highly valued by Native Americans for warfare and hunting. Horses were later essential to the exploration of the American frontier and were instrumental in shaping the nation. Many people relish the image of a cowboy traveling across America, the horse as his trusted companion. Horses were then used as valuable workers and as transportation, before becoming pets. To many Americans, eating a horse is taboo and would be like eating a cat or a dog.

It seems that's the end of the matter for now. So while there is an abundance of horses available for slaughter, horsemeat is cheap, horsemeat is tasty, and horsemeat is good for you, most Americans say, "Nay, nay, we just don't want to eat our friends."

⇨ Why Did Pirates Make People Walk the Plank Instead of Just Throwing Them Overboard?

According to Hollywood, the standard way to kill anyone on a pirate ship was to make them walk the plank. But given that it would be far quicker to just throw the victim overboard, did this really happen, or is it cinematic sensationalism?

There is some evidence that this barbaric practice did exist. Before his execution in 1769, a seaman named George Wood confessed to forcing a prisoner to walk the plank. Then, in 1829, the Dutch ship Vhan Fredericka was boarded by pirates near the Virgin Islands. The crew members were killed by having cannonballs tied to their feet and being made to walk overboard.

While there are not many other cases that are backed by historical records, the idea gained significant traction with the public in the 1800s, when writers began referring to the practice in literature. Robert Louis Stevenson's 1883 novel *Treasure Island* has a number of references to walking the plank.

It does seem that some pirates did engage in this method of prisoner disposal, but why?

Some say they did it to avoid the murder penalty, the idea being that the prisoner had killed himself. This is highly unlikely, as forcing a person to kill himself would be considered murder, and given that piracy was also a capital crime, what difference did it make, anyway?

Most historians agree that walking the plank was used for two reasons. It was done primarily as a sadistic form of entertainment for the pirates, and secondly, in order to inflict psychological torture on their prisoners, especially in cases where the victim was a disloyal crew member who was guilty of mutiny.

So, while walking the plank did occur, it was relatively rare, and more often than not, the pirates did just throw their victims overboard. So why does the perverse concept still exist in popular culture today? Maybe it was just too good to drown.

⇨ Why Does Glass Squeak When You Rub It?

Often when a person rubs a glass with a finger, a squeaking noise is produced. The noise that is made is a high-frequency vibration and is the result of the stick-and-slip nature of friction.

When you push one surface over another, friction resists the movement. Human skin is elastic, so as you push, the force will make tiny areas of your skin stretch and distort as it sticks to the glass. As the force of the push increases, a threshold is reached at which the friction is overcome and the skin, which was initially stuck to the glass, slips forward. The force required to move the finger then drops, and the skin springs back into shape as it slides along the glass before it again becomes stuck.

Once the skin is back to its normal shape, the friction increases once again, and the finger stops momentarily while the force distorts the skin again. This stick-and-slip phenomenon is like a chain reaction along your fingertip, similar to the ripples on a pond. A steady push across the glass will create hundreds of distortions per second, producing a vibration in the glass, which is amplified into audible sound waves.

It is not your skin that makes the noise, but the glass. The pitch depends on the shape and thickness of the glass, and the amount of friction between your finger and the glass.

⇨ Why Do Men Snore More than Women?

Humans are susceptible to snoring because we can speak. To facilitate complex speech in our ancestors, the voice box dropped down lower in the body than the tongue. Because of this "laryngeal descent," a space was created behind the tongue called the oropharynx. Like other muscles in our body, the tongue relaxes during sleep and can fall back into this space, especially when we lie on our backs.

So why is it that men tend to snore more than women?

Men's voice boxes are typically lower in the neck than female's, creating a larger space behind the tongue. This is also the reason men have

deeper voices. When a man's tongue relaxes during sleep, it falls back into that space and causes a partial obstruction. As the airway is only partially obstructed, his breathing will cause the soft tissues near the airway to vibrate, resulting in snoring.

With most women, the voice box is not as low, so the space behind the tongue is smaller. When the tongue falls back, it tends to block the entire airway, causing the woman to wake up rather than snore. This creates a vicious cycle, keeping men asleep and women awake.

So how much more do men snore? About twice as much. But what this really means is that both sexes try to snore, but only men are good at it.

⇨ How Did the Term "Gringo" Originate?

Gringo is a term used by a Latin American or Spaniard to refer to an English-speaking foreigner. It is generally applied to someone from the United States, particularly a white American. While originally used with neutral connotations, the word is now sometimes used by Hispanic Americans as a derogatory or racial term.

Some say that gringo owes its beginnings to the Mexican-American War, which began in 1846. The Mexican soldiers got tired of hearing the Americans continually singing "Green Grow the Rushes, O," a song based on a Robert Burns poem. As a result, the Mexicans began referring to the Americans as "Green Grows," which with their accent sounded like "gringos."

However, gringo was being used by the Spanish before that time, and most linguists believe it is a phonetic alteration of *griego*, the Spanish word for Greek. In Spanish, the expression *hablar en griego*, literally "to talk in Greek," means to speak unintelligibly. This phrase was being used since the late 1700s, where foreigners in Malaga, Spain, whose command of Spanish was poor, were called gringos by the locals. The same name was applied to the Irish in Madrid at the time, and it was soon used by the Spanish to refer to any foreigners.

⇨ Does Cucumber Relieve Puffy Eyes?

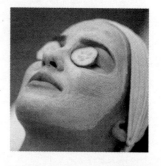

Puffy eyes are caused by various factors such as a lack of sleep, smoking, drinking, and genetics. And cucumbers have long been used to reduce the puffy appearance. One of the most commonly seen beauty treatments is women lying down with a piece of sliced cucumber over each eye. But does this peculiar method actually reduce puffiness around the eyes, or is it just the fact that the cucumbers feel nice because they're cold?

Cucumbers contain ascorbic acid and caffeic acid, two powerful antioxidants that inhibit the production of free radicals that can damage cells. The antioxidants in cucumbers are thought to reduce irritation and water retention around the eyes. These chemicals, along with the vitamin C that cucumbers contain, also help the slices to smooth the skin and reduce swelling.

The cucumber slices used on the eyes are usually chilled, so their cooling effects also help to reduce swelling while tightening the skin around the eyes. They are best applied for five to ten minutes.

While most beauticians agree that they do work, medical professionals generally say that the best way to reduce puffy eyes is a good night's sleep.

⇨ Does the Black Stuff Athletes Put Under Their Eyes Really Stop Glare?

Many American football players, baseball players, and other athletes apply grease or black strips, known as eye black, under their eyes in an attempt to reduce glare. This is done where stadium lights or sunlight can impair the player's vision and ability to see an airborne ball. Babe Ruth is believed to be the first sportsman to wear it in the 1930s.

The idea behind eye black is that it reduces the amount of glare that reaches your eyes, known as disability glare. Because black colors absorb most light frequencies, the theory is that excessive light from sources in our peripheral vision, such as the sun or stadium lights, will be absorbed by the black color. By placing the black just below the eyes, the disability glare  will be reduced, and the definition and contrast of the objects being looked at directly, such as a flying ball, will increase.

A number of studies have been conducted in recent years to determine whether eye black actually works, most notably at the University of New Hampshire and Yale University. The experiments had some limitations—in particular, the subjects may have subconsciously altered their responses because they knew what type of eye black they were wearing. The experiments all concluded that traditional eye grease, which is made of beeswax, paraffin, and carbon, does in fact reduce glare and improve contrast sensitivity, while petroleum jelly and anti-glare stickers had no impact. However, even with the eye grease, it was found that the glare reduction was fairly minimal. This led the researchers to question how much advantage the glare reduction actually gives players.

It seems that eye black does work to some extent, though, and it probably doesn't have any negative effects, so why not use it? Mind you, professional tennis players, who hit a very fast-moving ball in the sun or under lights, never wear eye black. Perhaps they don't feel the need to look so intimidating.

⇨ Why Are Inexperienced People Called Greenhorns?

A greenhorn is an inexperienced, gullible, or naïve person. The word is often used to describe someone who is new to an area and unaccustomed to its workings, such as a city person who has gone to a rural town to live. It is generally used in a derogatory manner, but how did it originate?

Some claim that greenhorn originated in the 15th century in reference to young oxen having new, or "green," horns. This seems a plausible explanation, but is not the likely derivation.

37

The word's likely beginnings are from a 17th century jewelry manufacturing process. Various pieces of jewelry at the time, in particular brooches, were made out of horn that was set into a silver frame. The horn was decorated by impressing a figure onto it. This was a delicate process, and the horn had to be heated to a specific temperature before it was shaped over the mold. If it was heated too high, the horn turned green and was rendered useless. This was a mistake common to inexperienced apprentices, who became known as greenhorns.

⇨ Is It Safe to Stand Close to Microwave Ovens?

A microwave oven cooks food by bombarding it with microwaves. Microwaves are radio waves that are used at a frequency of about 2,500 megahertz in ovens. At this frequency, the radio waves are absorbed by water, fat, and sugar molecules, all of which are  present in humans. Since most microwave ovens have clear glass doors that we can see through, is there any danger in standing nearby?

Both scientists and consumers have debated for years whether microwave radiation is dangerous, and in the absence of human testing, we don't know how much we can safely tolerate. Microwave radiation is non-ionizing, which means it can't change the molecular structure of something.

However, it is known that microwave radiation can heat body tissue in the same way it heats food, and an overexposure to it would be harmful, resulting in burning, damage to the eyes, and damage to the testes in males.

But the reason light can pass through the oven door but microwave radiation can't is the cooking chamber in the oven, known as a Faraday cage. It is a layer of conductive mesh on the inside of the glass door. The mesh is far narrower than microwave wavelengths, but much wider than light wavelengths. This means that the microwaves cannot pass through the door, but light can, which allows you to see the food.

Unless the oven is damaged or faulty and allows the microwaves to escape in large quantities, it is perfectly safe to be nearby. Government regulations actually allow for a certain amount of radiation to be leaked from an oven. The radiation level from any leak is likely to be minute, and it drops sharply with distance, so standing two feet away is probably safe, even with a faulty oven.

In short, proximity to a microwave oven is not dangerous. But as the saying goes, if you can't stand the heat, get out of the kitchen.

⇨ Do Steroids Shrink Men's Testicles?

Anabolic steroids are synthetic substances that have similar effects to testosterone on the human body. Testosterone is the male sex hormone produced naturally in the testicles, and is responsible for the growth of bones and muscles, as well as the development of masculine features. For years, it has been said that steroids makes a man's testicles shrink. But if a man gets more testosterone, wouldn't his sex organs increase in size?

No. One of the side effects of prolonged steroid use is testicular atrophy, or in layman's terms, ball shrinkage.

The human brain has a feedback system that regulates the body's hormones. When testosterone levels are low, it produces secondary hormones (LH and FSH) that send a message to the testicles telling them to increase testosterone production. Artificially increasing testosterone in the body to high levels sends a message to the brain that the body is producing too much testosterone. The body then attempts to correct this imbalance by suppressing testosterone production in the testicles.

The excess testosterone in the bloodstream is unable to transfer into the testicles, so they become dormant. This can result in a number of side effects, including loss of libido and smaller, nonfunctioning testes. The testicles start healthy, but over time, they begin to shrink from a lack of activity, eventually becoming very small.

So, the next time you see a powerfully built bodybuilder showing off and flexing his muscles, you can rest safe in the knowledge that while he's big, you're probably bigger.

⇨ Do Toads Cause Warts?

It has been an old wives' tale for decades that touching a toad will give you warts. This probably owes to the fact that most toads have wart-like lumps on their backs. Some people believe these lumps to be warts, or similar to warts, and fear they could be contagious if touched. There is even a species called the warty toad.

However, toads can't give you warts. Warts are caused by a human virus called the human papillomavirus, or HPV. Skin infections from HPV can cause noncancerous skin growths, known as warts. These warts are caused by a rapid growth of cells on the outer layer of the skin that can appear and regress spontaneously over the course of months, and can be passed from person to person by physical contact. Scientists believe that the likelihood of getting warts depends on the strength of an individual's immune system, and they are more common in children.

The "warts" on a toad's back are actually glands that produce and secrete toxins that the toad uses to ward off predators as its main defense mechanism. All toads have the glands, and some produce more toxic secretions than others, depending on the species. This poison can cause skin irritations in humans.

As kids generally get more warts, and they are more likely to handle (and torment) toads, this has served to fuel the myth.

⇨ Why Are Your Muscles Sorer Two Days After Exercise?

Most of us have experienced it at some point. You do some strenuous exercise that you haven't done for a while, and the next day you feel okay. Maybe you were fitter than you thought! But then the day after that, bang, you almost can't move.

This condition is called delayed onset muscle soreness, or DOMS. Also known as muscle fever, it is the pain and stiffness felt in muscles days after exercise. There are a number of theories as to what causes DOMS, including calcium accumulation in the damaged muscles, or a buildup of lactic acid, but the most widely accepted theory is that it is caused by eccentric (or lengthening) contractions of the muscles during exercise. These contractions cause microtrauma to the muscle fibers that stimulate pain receptors called nociceptors, which are located within the muscles and give the sensation of pain.

But why does the pain come on day two and not straight away?

The healing process, called the inflammatory response cascade, is the reason. This response is a series of events that takes place over a period of four to five days. The body immediately responds to the muscle trauma by releasing hormones called cytokines, which direct the cells in the injured muscles to heal. Other hormones called prostaglandins send extra blood to the affected muscles to aid in the repair. This process starts slowly during the first 24 hours, and it isn't until day two that it reaches its peak and the muscle cells begin repairing properly. During this time you'll feel pain in the form of sore muscles, a loss of range of motion, and reduced strength.

It is also usually on day two that you vow never to exercise again. Who knows, perhaps the inflammatory response cascade heals the bad memory you have of it as well, because there always seems to be a next time.

⇨ Why Are Airplane Cabin Lights Dimmed for Takeoff and Landing?

How many times does it happen? You're on a plane and in the middle of reading a key part of your book when an announcement is made that the plane is preparing to land and the cabin lights are about to be dimmed. You have to resort to that tiny light above your head, which frankly does nothing and shouldn't even be called a light. The pilot never explains the reason for this dimming and just says it is protocol for nighttime landings. Why do they do it?

The dimming of the lights during takeoff and landing could be the difference between life and death. Those times are considered the most critical and are when most accidents happen, so the lights are dimmed as a standard safety measure.

The purpose of dimming the lights is to match the cabin environment to the exterior environment. This is done to prepare for a potential evacuation in the dark. Going from a brightly lit cabin into the outside darkness would require a period of visual adjustment that could cost precious seconds. But with the lights already dimmed, the passengers' eyes would already be accustomed to the outside conditions, and this would facilitate a safer and faster escape. For example, with the eyes already adjusted, a passenger would be able to locate an exit or an evacuation slide more quickly.

This is also the reason why cabin window shades are raised. It assists with adjusting the passengers' eyes to the outside light, as well.

This is what all the airlines claim, anyway. The real reason is they just don't want you to finish your book.

⇨ Why Don't People Ride Zebras?

What's black and white and eats like a horse? A zebra. Zebras are very horse-like. They have manes and tails, eat grass, and are of a similar size and shape to horses. So, why don't we ride them?

Many people throughout history have attempted to tame, train, and ride zebras. The attempts proved both painstaking and dangerous. Most failed.

The main reason zebras can't be tamed is their aggressive disposition. Though domestic horses are known to kick and bite, zebras are different. When they kick, they look behind at their target, aiming and striking with power and purpose. They also lock on when they bite, holding on in an attempt to kill their foe. Zebras cause more injuries to zookeepers than any other animals do.

While the occasional single zebra has been partially tamed, it's proved impossible to domesticate herds. It is very difficult to lasso a zebra, as they watch the rope and duck their heads away at the last second. They are also

bad-tempered, nervous, and easily agitated, and run at the slightest provocation.

Given that zebras and horses share so many physical characteristics, why are horses so tolerant, but zebras aren't?

Evolution is the answer. While horses originated in the relatively safe environments of Asia and Europe, zebras evolved on the plains of Africa, sharing the space with many large predators such as lions, leopards, and crocodiles. Zebras are a prey species, so in order to survive, they developed intense early-warning mechanisms, making them extremely flighty. Their circumstances also made them violent; when cornered or attacked, they were forced to fight for their lives.

Zebras also evolved alongside early man, who used them as a food source. This means zebras inherently view people as a threat, and recent domestication attempts cannot undo millennia of conditioning. Horses, on the other hand, evolved in the absence of early man, so they do not see us as such a threat.

It is because of these evolutionary factors that you won't see people competing on zebras in equestrian events for a long time to come.

⇨ Why Do Girls Throw Like a Girl?

As a schoolboy, there is no more embarrassing taunt than being told that you throw like a girl. There are a lot of other disparaging ways that boys can be likened to girls, but what makes the throwing jibe so offensive?

It's because the "throwing gap," as it is known, is the biggest difference between the genders. Janet Hyde, a professor of psychology and women's studies at the University of Wisconsin, has studied the gender gap in detail across a wide array of skills, ranging from behavioral, psychological, communication, and physical. She found that men and women are very alike, far more than people believe, in all areas except for one: throwing. Based on standard deviations from the mean, she measured a variety of differences, including physical aggression (which was 0.60 standard deviations in favor of men—not high significance), and grip strength (which was 0.66 toward men—not high significance). But when it came to throwing velocity and throwing distance, the figures skewed markedly, and were well above anything else, both physical and psychological. Throwing speed was 2.18 standard deviations in favor of men, and distance was 1.98 in favor of men. Researchers at the US National Institute of Child Health and Human Development also found that men have a significantly better aim than women do when it comes to throwing.

So, how do girls throw? Girls throw with a slow, weak forearm motion and with a small step on the same side as the throwing hand, which actually negates forward thrust. Boys, on the other hand, use their whole body, stepping forward with the opposite foot, rotating with the hips and shoulders, and whipping with the arm and hand. This rotation is the key to power in a throw. In boys, the hips rotate forward, opening the body up, then the shoulders snap around. Girls, however, usually rotate their hips and shoulders together, resulting in a powerless throw.

Some claim that boys are better at throwing because they've practiced more from a young age or because of their superior strength, but in most societies, this does not seem to be the case. Before puberty, the physical differences between boys and girls are not enough to account for the throwing gap, and even at the age of four, the gap is three times greater than any other motor function. By age fifteen, nearly every boy throws better than the best girl does.

But what is the explanation for the throwing gap? Once again, it's evolution. Our early ancestors survived by hunting, and the most important trait for hunting was throwing, be it a spear or a rock. The man with the most powerful and accurate throw killed the most animals to feed his family, and his genes were more likely to be passed down. Women, on the other hand, did not hunt, so had no reason to develop good throwing skills.

⇨ Why Do Pharmacists Stand on Raised Platforms?

Unlike other retail stores, drugstores have a raised platform at the back where the pharmacist stands high above everybody else. Could there possibly be a reason for this strange design?

According to the pharmacists, there are a number of reasons.

1. The high platform aids in security. As all the prescription medications and poisons are kept with the pharmacist, the high counters discourage customers from entering that area to take or steal medications.

2. The raised platform gives the pharmacist an unobstructed view of the entire store. This helps him to detect shoplifters, monitor his employees, and assess if any customer might need help.

3. The pharmacist is usually the manager or owner of the store, and as they are often busy in the back, far away from the front counters, it gives them a visible prominence in the store.

4. If the drugstore was not originally built as a drugstore, it is easier and cheaper to run the required electrical cabling under a raised platform than putting it in the walls or roof.

5. A raised wooden platform is more comfortable for the pharmacist compared with a concrete-based floor. The pharmacist often stands for hours at a time, so this, they say, is a very important factor.

So there you have it. There are actually valid reasons for the raised platform, and it's not just because the pharmacists want to seem superior, go on a power trip, or are insecure because they didn't quite make it into medical school. But that doesn't answer this question: What do they wear those white medical smocks for?

⇨ Why Do People Seem More Attractive When You're Drunk?

The plight of the 21st century single male might sound familiar to some: You've been drinking all night when suddenly the bar is filled with gorgeous women. It looks like a model's convention in there, and the girl you're talking to really is beautiful. You look at her sparkling eyes and her winning smile. She's irresistible. You ask her home and she agrees. You can't believe your luck! That is, until you wake up the next day. "Surely, this isn't the girl I took home. This one could scare a hungry dog out of a butcher's shop. What was I thinking? What happened?" What happened was your beer goggles, the ultimate societal curse.

The phenomenon known as beer goggles means that the more alcohol you drink, the more attractive you find the opposite sex. Some say that it is just a myth, and alcohol merely suppresses people's inhibitions, making them less discriminating and more likely to approach strangers. Science says otherwise.

Results of a study done at the University of Bristol in England showed that a group of college students found members of the opposite sex 10 percent more attractive after drinking only two beers. Another study, done at the University of Glasgow and the University of St. Andrews, both in Scotland, found that students who had consumed a moderate amount of alcohol found the faces of members of the opposite sex 25 percent more attractive than when they were sober.

The leading theory as to what causes beer goggles is related to bilateral symmetry. One of the predominant factors of beauty is symmetry. A perfectly symmetrical face is generally found to be good-looking. This is because symmetry is a sign of health, suggesting that the person is free from disease and deformation. In simple terms, the more similar one side of a person's face is to the other side, the better looking that person is. A series of studies suggests that alcohol impairs our ability to perceive asymmetry, making us find asymmetrical faces far more attractive when drunk than when sober. So, it's not that our standards drop, but that our brain genuinely finds people more attractive during the time of intoxication.

But it's not just as simple as getting drunk to increase your chances—beer goggles do not bring success if applied unilaterally. To reap the benefits of the phenomenon, your target must also be drunk. Fortunately, the goggles fit both sexes. Note of caution: Studies have also found that beer goggles make the same sex seem more attractive, as well.

⇨ Are Bulls Really Attracted to the Color Red?

Bullfighting has been a tradition in Spain, France, and some Latin American countries for centuries. The matadors use a small red cape, known as a muleta, in the latter part of the fight, and the bull goes mad, charging at it repeatedly. Why does the color red make these animals so angry?

It doesn't. The bull is actually charging at the movement of the cape, not its color. Bulls, along with all bovines, are color blind to red, but they are bred to be aggressive and to charge any moving object. Tests have shown that bulls prefer to charge a person who is moving rather than someone who is stationary, regardless of the color they are wearing. The matadors entice the bull to charge by waving the red cape at it. This movement infuriates the bull and it charges. And the bulls will charge any color. In the early stages of the fight, the

matador uses a larger magenta- and gold-colored cape, and the bull charges that with equal fury.

So, if a bull can't see red, why is the muleta red?

The ornate costumes of the matadors and the red capes that they use are all part of the spectacle, and that has been the case since bullfighting began. They are considered an important part of the culture and tradition of bullfighting.

There is also a practical reason for the cape's color. The red helps mask the bull's blood.

⇨ How Did the Term "Johnson" Come to Mean a Man's Penis?

Men have been naming their penises for centuries. There is a written reference to "Jockum" being used as a name for the appendage way back in the 1500s. But how did Johnson come about?

Some claim that it began with R. G. Johnson, a man who made baseball bats at his Sebago Bat Company in the 1940s. He always burned his name onto the bats, which were referred to as "Johnsons." Given the phallic shape of the bats, the word was then used as a euphemism for penis.

Others say that it began in the 1960s when Lyndon Johnson was the US president. Some people thought he was a "dick," and so used his name for this purpose.

Both of these suggestions are incorrect; the term actually began in the 1800s.

Johnson is thought to be based on "John Thomas," the British slang word for penis, which dates from the mid-19th century. That term was popularized by the English novelist D. H. Lawrence in his controversial 1928 book *Lady Chatterley's Lover*. In that book, the main character refers to his own penis as John Thomas.

Historians are not sure how that term initially came to refer to the penis, but Johnson developed from it and has been used, particularly in the United States, ever since. Perhaps men figured that because the penis was ruling their lives, it was only right to give it a name.

⇨ Why Are the Words on the Back Cover of a Book Called a Blurb?

A blurb is a promotional description, often found on the back jacket cover of a book.

The word blurb was coined by the American humorist and illustrator, Gelett Burgess. In 1907, Burgess's book *Are You a Bromide?* was presented in a limited edition to guests at an annual trade association dinner. It was customary for copies at such events to have a special dust jacket, and Burgess decided to provide an illustration.

The jackets of many serious novels at the time pictured a heroine in some sort of pose, and Burgess drew a parody of this for his book: a particularly buxom blonde with the label "Miss Belinda Blurb." Above the picture were the words "YES, this is a 'BLURB'!" and Belinda was described as being "in the act of blurbing."

It is not known why Burgess picked the name "Blurb," but it stuck, and came to refer to the text on the back cover of any book.

⇨ What Are the Origins of the Molotov Cocktail?

A Molotov cocktail is an improvised handheld firebomb, often thrown by rioters or protesters at police.

The term "Molotov cocktail" originated during World War II. The phrase was invented by the Finnish, who were referring to the Soviet foreign minister Vyacheslav Molotov. He was responsible for the partitioning of Finland under a pact with Nazi Germany, and many believed he was also responsible for the subsequent invasion of Finland in November 1939.

There was much propaganda associated with the invasion, including the ludicrous claim by Molotov that the bombing missions were actually humanitarian food deliveries for the starving Finns.

In response to this, the Finns referred to the Soviet cluster bombs as "Molotov bread baskets." When the Finns developed handheld petrol bombs to throw at the Soviet tanks, they called them Molotov cocktails, describing them as a "drink to go with the food."

▷ Why Do We Have Leap Years?

A leap year, also known as an intercalary year, occurs about every four years to synchronize the calendar year with the solar year. Pretty simple, right? Sort of.

The solar year is the length of time it takes the earth to complete one orbit of the sun, which is approximately 365.2425 days. As the calendar year is only 365 days, an extra day is added to February, the shortest month, about every four years. If this variance weren't adjusted for, we would lose almost six hours from each calendar year, which after 100 years would amount to 24 days.

The four-year model was adopted in the Julian calendar, introduced by Julius Caesar in 45 BC. However, the length of the solar year is slightly less than 365¼ days—less by 11 minutes. To compensate for this discrepancy, Pope Gregory XIII introduced the Gregorian calendar in 1582. This is the calendar we currently use, and it omits a leap year three times every 400 years. A century year is not a leap year unless it is divisible by 400—so 1700, 1800, and 1900 were not leaps years, but 1600 and 2000 were. This more closely equates the calendar and solar years, and using this method, it will take more than 3,000 years for the calendar year to gain one extra day.

The term "leap year" comes from the fact that a fixed date in the calendar advances one day of the week each year. That is, if your birthday was on a Tuesday this year, it'll be on a Wednesday next year. But in the 12 months following a leap day (from March 1 to February 28), a date will advance by two days, thus "leaping" over a day.

The chance of being born on a leap day is about 1 in 1,500, and there are various traditions associated with leap years. In Britain, it is said that women can only propose marriage in leap years, while in Greece, marriage in a leap year is considered unlucky.

Leap days have other costs and benefits. If you're an employee being paid a salary and it falls mid-week, it's an extra day you have to work for no money. Bad for you, good for your boss. If your birthday falls on a leap day, you should only get presents every four years, but then you will technically age four times more slowly than the rest of us.

⇨ Do Sharks Have to Keep Swimming to Stay Alive?

Take a visit to any large aquarium that has sharks, and you're sure to hear people saying with confidence that sharks have to keep swimming to stay alive, and if they stop, they'll die. Is there any truth to this?

Like other fish, sharks breathe through their gills, which are respiratory organs equivalent to our lungs. As water passes over the gill membranes, blood vessels extract oxygen from the water. How the sharks force the water over their gills differs among the species.

Most sharks (about 94 percent of the 400 species) don't have to constantly swim to stay alive. These older species use a process called buccal pumping, named after the cheek muscles they use to physically filter water into their mouths and over their gills. These sharks, which include the nurse

and bullhead sharks, can alternate between swimming and rest.

As sharks evolved and became more active, this method of pumping water became secondary, and it was more efficient to simply take in water while swimming. This method of breathing is known as ram ventilation—the shark "rams" water into its open mouth while it swims and the water flows over its gills.

While some sharks, such as the sand tiger shark, can alternate between these two techniques, about two dozen species rely on ram ventilation. They have lost the buccal pumping anatomy, and they must keep swimming in order to stay alive. Apart from stopping briefly from time to time, these sharks would die from a lack of oxygen if they stopped swimming for a longer period.

Sharks that must constantly swim include the great white, the whale shark, and the mako shark. Don't feel too sorry for them, though; it's actually less work for these sharks to swim than to remain still.

⇨ Why Are Bugs Attracted to Light?

It's a gorgeous summer evening, and you decide to sit outside in the cool air to soak up the atmosphere. You turn the outdoor light on and the ambience is ruined within minutes as you are inundated with

thousands of bugs frantically swarming and flying at the light. Why do bugs go into such a fervor with lights? There are a number of theories to explain this often-suicidal entomological behavior, but no single scientific explanation has been agreed upon. In fact, it's one of the most disputed phenomena in the natural world.

The most popular theory to account for positive phototaxis in insects (that is, the attraction to light) is that the light interferes with their internal navigation systems. A number of insects, particularly moths, are thought to migrate and travel long distances using the moon to navigate, it being a relatively stationary reference point from which to gauge direction. They are able to travel in straight lines by maintaining a constant angle to the moon. When the insect mistakes an artificial light source for the moon, it continues to keep a constant angle to the light, but because of its close proximity, the insect spirals toward the light in a confused state.

Another theory claims that artificial lights confuse insects into thinking it's daytime, and since light allows them to hunt and avoid obstacles, they fly straight toward it. Others think the light source is seen as an emergency beacon, which the insects instinctively head for because the light is higher than their current, supposedly dangerous, position. Still another theory suggests that because of a peculiarity in their vision, insects perceive the darkest place in the sky to be an area of about one foot from the light source. As a safety mechanism to remain hidden, they seek out this darkest place and remain there, causing them to frantically circle the light within the dark band.

In a more novel explanation, some scientists claim that since many flowers reflect UV light, bugs may be attracted to artificial light sources that emit UV because they mistake them for a flower, a source of food. Supporting this is the fact that bugs tend to be more attracted to UV lights than to lights with longer wavelengths, such as red and yellow lights.

More intriguing still is the suggestion from one entomologist that moths actually mistake certain light sources for female moths. He discovered that the infrared light given off by candle flames shares common frequencies with the light given off by the pheromones in female moths, these pheromones being slightly luminescent. However, detracting from this theory is the fact that insects are far more attracted to UV than infrared light.

The final word: Nobody knows for sure.

▷ Do Pregnant Women Really Glow?

How many times have you heard it? "Have you seen her lately? She's pregnant, and really glowing." Is this an old wives' tale, or do women really glow when they're pregnant?

Many physiological changes occur to women while they're pregnant, and the pregnancy glow is actually one of them. The glowing effect on a woman's face is caused by a number of factors.

An influx of hormones, particularly progesterone, causes a pregnant woman's glands to produce more oil. This can make the face look shiny, softer, smoother, and more moisturized. During pregnancy, the skin also retains more moisture. This plumps it up, smoothing out fine lines and wrinkles.

Another key contributing factor is an increase in blood flow. During pregnancy, the body increases the production of blood by about 50 percent. This results in more blood circulating closer to the surface of the skin, leading to a brighter, fuller, and more radiant face—the glow.

But it's not all good news, ladies. The downsides from glow-contributing factors include hot flashes from the increased blood flow, puffiness from the water retention, and acne from the increased oil production and hormonal changes.

⇨ Why Do Roller Coasters Make You Puke?

People pay good money to go to amusement parks, eager to ride the roller coaster, the key attraction there. The bigger and faster, the better. Minutes later, they feel nauseated and begin puking everywhere. These rides are meant to be fun, so why can roller coasters make even the strongest of people vomit?

Motion sickness is the culprit. Also known as kinetosis, this is the feeling you get when the motion you sense in your inner ear is different from the motion you visually perceive.

Motion sensed in the brain comes from signals sent from the inner ear and the eyes. When we move intentionally, these signals are coordinated in the brain. However, when our movements are unintentional, like they are on a jerking and spinning roller coaster, the brain receives conflicting signals.

The inner ear signals come from the vestibular system. This system consists of canals that contain hair-like sensory nerve cells, as well as a fluid called endolymph. Because of inertia, endolymph resists any change in motion. When we spin around, the endolymph lags behind and stimulates the hair cells to signal to the brain that the head is spinning. As the endolymph starts to move at the same rate as you are spinning, it no longer stimulates the hair cells, and the brain adapts. When the spinning stops, the endolymph continues to move and this again stimulates the hair cells, which indicate to the brain that the spinning is still occurring. These incorrect signals contradict what the eyes are telling the brain

and cause dizziness, as if you were still spinning. This can result in a feeling of sickness.

But why do we sometimes vomit? There are two biological hypotheses for this unsavory by-product of roller coaster "fun."

When the brain senses a discord between vision and balance, it thinks that the person is hallucinating and that the hallucination is caused by a toxin in the system. As a defense mechanism to eliminate any dangerous poison, the brain forces the body to vomit.

Another theory is related to the body's fight-or-flight response to danger. When we experience unusual motions and dizziness, the heart pumps faster and redirects blood flow to our vital organs as a survival technique. The body empties its stomach contents so that the blood normally used in the digestion process can also be used by the vital organs.

Various techniques can be adopted to reduce the motion sickness caused by a roller coaster. These include taking regular and controlled breaths, having frequent exposure to the ride in order to increase your tolerance, and using the power of positive thinking—for example, if you think it'll be fun and won't make you sick, a self-fulfilling prophecy may result. But by far, the best way to avoid the feeling of nausea is to sit at the front of the roller coaster. This allows you to better anticipate the changes in direction so that your brain can adapt to them and not be tricked. And sitting at the front has another key advantage: It prevents you from getting covered in the puke from other people.

⇨ Why Are the Letters "YKK" on Many Clothes Zippers?

If you look down at the zipper on your pants, there's a fair chance it will bear the initials YKK—a more than 50 percent chance, in fact. Why?

The letters stand for Yoshida Kogyo Kabushikikaisha, a name that translates to Yoshida Manufacturing Shareholding Company, or the YKK Group.

In 1934, a shrewd business-man in Tokyo named Tadao Yoshida founded the company. He focused on just one simple product: the zipper. Not glamorous, but highly profitable. The company grew to become the world's largest zipper manufac-

turer, making over half the zippers on earth—more than seven billion a year. They have factories in 71 countries, with the largest, in Georgia, making over seven million zippers every day.

Yoshida was a very hands-on owner and practiced what he called the Cycle of Goodness. The fundamental tenet of the policy was that "no one prospers unless he renders benefit to others." Using this principle, he strove to make high-quality, durable zippers that were the best on the market. He succeeded.

So the next time you're zipping up, take a moment to think of Mr. Yoshida. Don't daydream too much, though. A mistake concerning multiple fastening metal teeth in that vicinity could be very costly.

⇨ Why Is There No Cure for the Common Cold?

The common cold is a mild viral disease that infects the nose, throat, and respiratory system. It generally results in nasal congestion, sneezing, coughing, and breathing difficulties.

The cold is the most common disease from which humans suffer, with most people getting at least one or two colds every year. As a group, it is estimated that Americans experience about one billion colds every year, which has a marked effect on the economy. Given that medical science has eradicated smallpox and polio, created vaccines for measles and mumps, and extended average life expectancy, people often rightly ask, "Why can't we cure the common cold?"

A cold is a general term for over 200 viruses that can infect the body. The most common are the rhinoviruses, and even they have over 100 strains. The viruses enter the cells in the nose, where they multiply and rapidly mutate in the human host to form new viruses.

The number and nature of these viruses make vaccination impractical.

Curing the cold would mean creating a single vaccine that would be effective for more than 200 viruses, as a generalized rhinovirus vaccine would not protect against other types of viruses. Even creating a rhinovirus vaccine would be difficult, as there are usually up to 30 types of that virus circulating at any time, and only around 10 percent of those will be present the following year. Health officials are unable to predict which virus types will be prevalent each year. And because of the mutative abilities of the cold viruses, even if a vaccine could be created, it likely would no longer be useful by the time it was developed.

Only humans show cold-like symptoms, which rules out animal testing. And to test humans, a rhinovirus would have to be found that the subjects had not already been exposed to, which would be an almost impossible task.

The likely end result of all this is that when science has cured every other disease and we're all living until we're 300, the common cold will be just as common as it is today.

⇨ What Causes Songs to Get Stuck in Our Heads?

You're driving to work listening to the radio, when Lady Gaga's "Poker Face" comes on. By the time you make it to work, you're singing her incredibly catchy chorus in your head over and over. This lasts all day; you hum it, tap it out on the desk, and sing the song repeatedly until it drives you crazy. Sound familiar?  What causes a tune like this to get stuck in our heads, forcing us to play it over and over and over again?

It's an earworm. Sometimes known as stuck song syndrome, an earworm is a catchy piece of music that plays in a continuous loop in a person's mind long after they stop listening to the song. The term is translated from the German word *ohrwurm*. They usually last between 15 and 30 seconds, and 99 percent of people fall victim to earworms on a regular basis.

Music cognition research suggests that earworms are related to the brain's motor cortex. There is a lot of activity in that part of the brain when people listen to music, and the brain often sings along as an imaginary participant. The problem is, the brain keeps singing long after the music stops.

Earworms tend to be a small fragment or chorus of a song, and are usually songs we've been repeatedly exposed to recently. However, they can also be caused by experiences that trigger the memory of a song. The songs usually have simple and repetitive lyrics and an upbeat melody, but with an unexpected variation in rhythm that piques the listener's interest—essentially, the same factors that make certain pop songs and jingles successful in the first place. Songs with lyrics account for the vast majority of earworms.

Most people are doing something routine and not concentrating on a particular task when earworms strike. You are also more likely to get one when you're stressed, tired, or idle, and research has found that people who are neurotic or obsessive compulsive experience them more often.

So, what's the point of these persistent little critters? Some experts claim they assist in emotional regulation, while others suggest they are a way of keeping an idle brain busy. There is also the suggestion that earworms have an evolutionary origin. Before writing was invented, songs helped people to remember and then share information. Supporting this theory is the fact that when people sing their earworms aloud, they are usually a surprisingly close match to the original song in terms of pitch, key, and rhythm.

Given that we can now write stuff down and don't have to rely on melodic mnemonics, how do you get rid of an earworm? That's the problem: They're notoriously difficult to dislodge, and the harder we try to suppress them, the more entrenched they often become. They usually crawl out on their own eventually, but some proven cures are to sing or listen to another song, do an activity that involves more concentration, or listen to the entire song a few times in an attempt to exhaust it. One study suggested that chewing gum might also help. Whatever you do, don't tell a friend about it, as that'll give them the same earworm and they'll hate you for the rest of the day.

So, which songs cause the most earworms? "Don't Worry, Be Happy" and "I Will Survive" are commonly cited as two of the biggest culprits. Kylie Minogue's "Can't Get You out of My Head" is also a repeat offender—it's so bad, in fact, that she wrote a song about it.

⇨ Are Women Better Multitaskers Than Men?

Multitasking is the ability to perform more than one task simultaneously or over a short period. Much to the chagrin of men, the idea that women are better multitaskers has been a long-held societal belief.

While people may become better at multitasking through practice, most experts who believe that women have an enhanced ability put it down to the evolutionary hunter-gatherer hypothesis. This theory says that while our male ancestors typically focused on one linear task at a time, such as hunting, women had to juggle a number of tasks, like gathering food, preparing meals, and tending to infant children. These skills were passed down over thousands of years so the brains of today's women are wired to be better at multitasking.

Critics of this theory, who are mostly men, say that the evidence to support it is purely anecdotal, and a number of the studies carried out on the topic are inconclusive or do not reflect real-life conditions. Indeed, one Swedish study found that men actually outperformed women in this area.

But in 2013, a group of psychologists from the University of Hertfordshire, the University of Glasgow, and the University of Leeds, all in Britain, conducted two detailed experiments, determined to find out the truth. Led by Dr. Gijsbert Stoet, in the first experiment they compared 120 men and 120 women in a computer test that involved switching between tasks involving shape-recognition and counting. The sexes performed equally when the tasks were done one at a time, but when the tasks were mixed up, a clear difference appeared. All the subjects slowed down and made more mistakes, but the men were significantly slower, taking 77 percent longer to respond, compared to the women, who took 69 percent longer.

The second test was more practical. The subjects were given eight minutes to complete a series of tasks, including answering a ringing phone, doing simple math problems, locating restaurants on a map, and deciding how to search for a lost key in a field. It was impossible to complete all the tasks in the allotted time, so it forced the subjects to prioritize and remain calm under stress. On the whole, the women out-performed the men, and in the lost key task in particular, they scored much higher. While the men were seen to act impulsively, the women were observed to possess a higher level of cognitive control than the men were, planning and organizing better when under pressure.

In the end, the researchers concluded that while some men are experts in the field, the average woman is better able to organize her time and switch quickly between tasks than the average man—that is, she is better at multitasking.

⇨ Why Do People Have Earlobes?

Situated at the base of the ear, sometimes attached and sometimes hanging freely, the human earlobe is composed of tough tissue. Earlobes are not considered to have any biological function, which begs the question, why do we even have them?

A number of evolutionary purposes have been put forward for the earlobe.

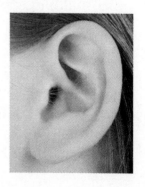

1. As the earlobe does not contain cartilage but is solely tissue, it has a large blood supply. It may have evolved in this way to help warm the ears and assist with balance.

2. The earlobes of our early ancestors may have had a more significant function. Perhaps they helped funnel sound into the ear or helped with movement of the ear, similar to the way a cat can move its ears to face the direction of the sound. This is something that might have been more important many years ago to allow us to better detect sounds.

3. In his 1967 book *The Naked Ape*, Desmond Morris postulated that, as the earlobe contains many nerve endings, it developed as an erogenous zone to augment the sexual experience in early humans. This, he claims, would have promoted monogamous "pair bonding," something that is essential to keep a couple together long enough to rear and nurture their offspring.

It is likely that we will never know the real answer as to why we have the lobes, but if the trend of wearing earrings continues, with the vast array of shapes and sizes available, it is possible that in thousands of years our lobes will have evolved to be much larger and more prominent than they are today.

⇨ If the Third Electrical Prong Is for Grounding, Why Don't All Plugs Have It?

Some plugs have them, some plugs don't. It is said that the third prong is to ground a device to stop electrocution. Wouldn't it be pretty essential to always have that prong?

First, let's look at how an electrical device is powered. To provide a source of power, electricity must flow in a circuit. In a typical American power outlet, the circuit consists of a right vertical slot that is connected to the "hot" wire, which has electricity flowing through it, and a left vertical slot that is connected to the "neutral" wire, which has no electricity. When a device is plugged in, it completes the circuit and the power flows through the device, as well.

The third prong is the "ground" wire, which is connected to earth in the main breaker box of your house. The ground wire does not carry any current and is not connected to the circuit. It connects the external conductive parts of the device to the earth, and in the normal operation of the device, is completely unnecessary—unless something goes wrong.

Where there is no third prong, if a hot wire comes loose inside the device and touches its metal casing, the device becomes hot, and anyone who touches it will receive a potentially fatal electric shock. In that case, the person becomes the path to the earth, and a surge of electricity will pass through the person to the breaker box in the house. Where the third prong does exist, it grounds the device, so the electricity will pass from the metal casing of the device through the ground wire and not through you.

The plugs on most electrical appliances with outer metal cases such as cookers, refrigerators, and toasters will have a third prong. The reason some appliances such as vacuum cleaners don't have a third prong or ground wire is that they have plastic casings with at least two layers of insulation between the conductive components of the device and any part that you are likely to touch. This additional insulation renders the ground wire unnecessary.

⇨ Is It True That You Can't Die in a Dream?

Many people have dreams in which they are about to die, but then they wake up just before their death occurs. This has led to the belief by some that you can't actually die in your dreams. Is there any basis to this, or is it an urban myth?

According to the International Association for the Study of Dreams, the idea that you can't die in your dreams, or that if you do you would have to die in real life as well, is a complete myth. They claim that many people have dreamed of their deaths and lived to tell the tale.

But there is another, more philosophical argument against the idea. To know that you are dead in your dream, you would have to be viewing the event, which means that you wouldn't be dead. Only the character you are "playing" in the dream can die, and not you as a spectator. Technically, this means you cannot die in a dream, but it is a fine line.

Many people report waking up before dying, but never actually dying in a dream. The reason this happens could be that people don't really understand what happens when our bodies die, and, as we have obviously never personally experienced death in real life, our minds do not have enough information to complete the event in a dream.

When interpreting dreams of death that do occur, some psychologists and dream experts say these dreams symbolically signify the ending of something in your actual life, such as a relationship. Others claim they are a positive thing, symbolizing inner changes or a transformation that is about to take place in your life.

One thing is for sure: If you do die in a dream, it doesn't mean that you have to actually die or are about to die in real life. So whether you die in your dreams or not, don't lose too much sleep over it.

⇨ What's the Difference Between a Turtle and a Tortoise?

Tortoises and turtles look very similar. They are both encased in a hard shell, and both have the major characteristics of reptiles—they are cold-blooded, breathe air, lay eggs on land, and have scales. They are both reptiles from the order of Testudines, but are in different classification families. A lot of people confuse the two animals, leading some to ponder, how do you tell them apart?

There are three main differences.

1. The key difference is that tortoises dwell on land, while turtles live in water most or all of the time, usually only coming on to land to lay eggs.

2. Because of their different habitats, the animals have adapted differently. Turtles are streamlined for swimming, with webbed feet or, in the case of sea turtles, long flippers. Their shells are flatter and hug their bodies

more. Tortoises, on the other hand, are not good swimmers and have stubby, column-shaped feet that assist them in traveling across land. They are not as streamlined as turtles and have high, domed shells. They also have sharp claws that they use to dig burrows for sleeping or shelter.

3. Turtles are omnivores. Sea turtles eat small invertebrates, as well as sea vegetation, and freshwater turtles eat plants, small fish, and insects. Tortoises are herbivores, eating grasses, low-lying shrubs, weeds, and any other vegetation.

Actually, there's one other major difference. While tortoises are known to compete in endurance races against sleepy hares, when turtles reach their teenage years, they often mutate and develop highly advanced ninja skills.

⇨ Why Is a Person's Signature Called Their "John Hancock"?

John Hancock was an American merchant and diplomat who lived from 1737 to 1793. He was the Governor of Massachusetts and president of the Second Continental Congress. He's known to more

people now than he was almost 300 years ago, because his name has become synonymous with any signature. "Just put your John Hancock here and the deal will be done." Why do people say things like that?

Because John Hancock had a massive signature, and he was proud of it.

Hancock was one of the men to sign the American Declaration of Independence in 1776. His flamboyant signature is by far the largest on the document, measuring nearly five inches long. It is told that when he signed the document he said with a laugh, "There—I guess King George or John Bull will be able to read that without his spectacles."

And that's why your signature today is called your John Hancock.

⇨ Did the Hanging Gardens of Babylon Ever Exist?

The Hanging Gardens of Babylon are one of the Seven Wonders of the Ancient World. They were built in 600 BC in the ancient city of Babylon, near present-day Hillah in Iraq. Destroyed in the 1st century AD by a number of earthquakes, the Gardens were an intricate multilayered terrace of flora and water features. The Gardens are said to have been built by the Neo-Babylonian king Nebuchadnezzar II to please his homesick wife, Amytis of Media. One source wrote of the Gardens: "In this palace he erected very high walks, supported by stone pillars; and by planting what was called a pensile paradise, and replenishing it with all sorts of trees, he rendered the prospect an exact resemblance of a mountainous country. This he did to gratify his queen, because she had been brought up in Media, and was fond of a mountainous situation."

But did any of this really happen, and did the Gardens actually exist?

There is no archaeological evidence whatsoever of the Gardens' existence. Of the Seven Wonders, it is the only one whose location has not been definitively established. It is possible that evidence exists beneath the Euphrates, but the river cannot be safely excavated to find out.

There is also a lack of documentary evidence supporting the existence of the Gardens. It was the Babylonian priest, Berossus, who credited the Gardens to King Nebuchadnezzar II when writing in 290 BC, but this was 300 years after their apparent creation. There is very little contemporaneous written evidence, and there is no mention of the King's wife. Many records of the King's works from the time exist, including detailed inscriptions, but none of these mention the elaborate Gardens. Herodotus, the Greek historian who lived in the 5th century BC, describes Babylon in his 440 BC work *Histories*, but there is no mention of the Gardens.

Adding to the skepticism, estimates based on descriptions of the Gardens state that they would have required at least 8,200 gallons of water per day to be sustainable.

Because of this lack of physical or documentary evidence, it has been suggested that the Gardens did not exist at all, and the descriptions found in the works of ancient Roman and Greek writers, including Diodorus Siculus, Quintus Curtius Rufus, and Strabo, are nothing more than a poetic creation.

⇨ Why Do People Look Upward When Thinking?

Ask someone a difficult question, and chances are they will either close their eyes or look up to the sky. Why is this so?

As with many conundrums such as this, there are a number of theories.

Many people use visualization to answer questions. If the eyes are open and receiving additional input, it is harder to concentrate and visualize the answer because the brain is busy dealing with the new information the eyes are seeing. People also have difficulty doing more than one thing at a time, so if they close their eyes or look upward, they are able to eliminate distractions and disengage from the world. By doing this, they can more easily access memories or focus their attention on the problem at hand.

This distraction theory was supported by a 2011 study by Annelies Vredeveldt, Graham Hitch, and Alan Baddeley at the University of York in England. Subjects watched a television show and were then asked questions about what they had seen and heard. One group answered

the questions while looking at a blank computer screen, while a second group answered with their eyes closed. A third group answered while watching a computer screen when images were shown on it, and the fourth group was distracted by a foreign language while they answered the questions. The people from the groups who looked at the blank screen or closed their eyes had far better recall than the people from the two groups who were distracted.

A second, more controversial theory to explain why people look up when they're thinking was postulated in the 1960s by a Canadian psychologist named Paul Bakan. He suggested that activity in certain parts of the brain could spill over into an adjacent region called the lateral eye field, which coordinates eye movements. He proposed that different kinds of thinking could automatically trigger lateral eye movements, or LEMs. When right-handed people are visualizing constructed events (that is, lying), they access the creative part of their brain and tend to look up and to the right. When they are recalling an actual memory (that is, being honest), they access the memory center of their brain and tend to look up and to the left. It is the opposite for left-handers.

This theory has been widespread for years, but a number of subsequent studies on LEMs have proved inconclusive. In 2012, a comprehensive three-part study on the topic was undertaken by Professor Richard Wiseman of the University of Hertfordshire in England. He found that there was no relationship between lying and eye movements.

If Wiseman is right, the probable reason that people look upward when thinking is to aid in concentration by eliminating distractions. But maybe they're just looking for a skywriter to give them a believable response.

⇨ What Is a Black Hole?

Don't let the name deceive you—a black hole is the opposite of empty space. It's only called that because we can't see it. And here's why.

A black hole is a place in space where the gravity is so strong that nothing can escape it, not even light. When a star gets to the end of its life cycle, its gravity can become so powerful that it collapses in upon itself, producing a super-nova explosion. Fragments of the star scatter through space, but a small and dense core will remain and compress into a smaller space. If the core's mass is large and dense enough (at least three times the size of the sun), its gravity will be so strong that a black hole develops, from which nothing can escape. The black hole can then continue to grow by using its gravity to absorb additional mass from its surroundings.

Black holes vary in size. They range from the size of an atom, to a stellar black hole that can be twenty times the mass of the sun, to a supermassive black hole that can reach a mass the size of millions of suns. Scientists believe there are as many as a billion stellar black holes in the Milky Way alone (which is the earth's galaxy), and they have discovered a supermassive black hole at its center, called Sagittarius A. It has a mass equal to four million suns.

So, given that we can't see them and no light can escape from them, how do we know they're there?

Scientists are able to detect black holes by watching their effects on other stars and gases. Nearby stars may be sucked into a black hole, or, if far enough away, orbit the black hole. As a star is drawn toward a black hole, it accelerates and heats up, emitting X-rays that scientists can see.

The term was first used in 1964, but the concept of black holes has been around for centuries, and Einstein discussed them in his theory of general relativity. But the key question is, could the earth be sucked into one?

No. The sun is not big enough to turn into a black hole, and there are no other black holes close enough to affect us.

⇨ How Did the Golfing Term "Birdie" Originate?

In the sport of golf, a birdie is a score of one stroke under par for any particular hole. As the term doesn't seem to relate in any way to the score or the game, it has led some people to wonder where it originated.

The term birdie began at the Atlantic City Country Club in New Jersey in 1899. Brothers Ab Smith and William Poultney Smith were golfing with George Crump, who later built the Pine Valley Golf Club. On one of the par-four holes, Crump hit his second shot to within inches of the cup. The Smith brothers exclaimed, "That was a bird of a shot!" and Crump's easy putt left him one under par for the hole.

The word "bird" had been used as slang in America since the early 1800s. Taken from 13th-century England, it was used to describe a person or thing of excellence.

The three men decided to call the score a birdie. This spread around the club, and with the many out-of-town visitors the club received, the word was soon being used around America, and then the world.

Some claim it was one of the Smith brothers who hit the shot, or that the ball actually hit a bird in flight before landing near the hole. Both of these claims are incorrect.

⇨ Do Animals Ever Commit Suicide?

Animal suicide refers to any self-destructive behavior displayed by animals that results in death. It is a controversial topic, and though there are examples of animals killing themselves, can these cases be technically classified as suicide, or is that a misnomer?

The issue of whether animals kill themselves has been debated for centuries. In the 2nd century AD, the Greek scholar Claudius Aelian wrote of a number of animal suicides, including an eagle that sacrificed itself by burning on the pyre of its dead master, a dolphin who was willingly captured, and dogs who starved to death after their owners had died.

In 1845, it was reported in London that a Newfoundland dog, after acting less lively for a number of days, threw himself into the water and tried to sink by remaining perfectly still. Each time he was rescued, he did it again until he finally held his head underwater and died. In other canine-related incidents, many dogs have been known to leap to their death from Overtoun Bridge in Scotland, and people classed this as suicide. But it was later discovered that the bridge was above a mink nesting ground, and the dogs were attracted to the scent, not realizing the consequences of their actions.

A certain species of ant is known to explode at will when threatened, emitting a poisonous substance when they do. While they are intentionally killing themselves, they are doing so to protect the colony, much like a soldier who takes a massive risk in a war situation. Some bees will also remove themselves from a hive if they know they're infected with a disease. This makes them die faster, but they are sacrificing themselves for the good of the hive. Some mother spiders let their young eat them, but this, too, is an act of altruism, ensuring the survival of their offspring by providing a nutritious meal.

While it is accepted that animals can suffer from mental health issues, and feel stressed and depressed, the question hinges on their intent. To be classed as suicide, the killing must be done intentionally, and the animal must know that its actions will end its life. This requires the ability to understand its own mortality, which is something many scientists believe is uniquely human.

Antonio Preti, a psychiatrist at the University of Cagliari in Italy, has examined around 1,000 studies published over 40 years. He claims to have found no evidence of an animal knowingly attempting suicide in the wild. He believes that any seemingly intentional deaths in captivity are caused by unnatural behavior triggered by the stress of being imprisoned, or by the animal trying to escape. He describes the cases in Claudius Aelian's ancient book as "anthropomorphic fables."

But what about lemmings, you may ask? Everybody knows that they kill themselves en masse by jumping off cliffs. Actually, they don't. These small, misunderstood rodents migrate in large groups and often choose to leap off cliffs into rivers to find new habitats. While they can swim, sometimes they overestimate their abilities and drown.

⇨ Is It Possible for Robots to Think for Themselves?

Is the dreaded science fiction scenario possible? Humans are subjugated to robots, following their every command as they rule the world, self-improve, and do whatever they like.

While this sounds unrealistic, experts say that advances in technology may have made the thinking robot possible.

Until recently, humans have operated robots by either remote control or specific verbal commands that the robot is programmed to compute. But now, increasingly autonomous machines, such as toys or vacuum cleaners that clean the room alone without needing any human instructions, are available. Manufacturers predict that this sort of machine will advance further in the next five years, so that robots are able to mind children and work in care homes and prisons, transmitting their progress to humans via built-in cameras.

Some incredible robots already exist. A system of software algorithms called Deep Q-Networks has been developed to play classic Atari games, such as Space Invaders, using only information about the pixels on a screen and the scoring method. The system is able to learn directly from its experience using trial and error, without further human interaction.

Then there's the Hasegawa Group at the Tokyo Institute of Technology. Using a technology called "Self-Organizing Incremental Neural Network," they have created robots that are capable of learning for themselves when they encounter problems that they have never seen before. The robots make educated guesses and decisions based on their experiences, enabling them to adapt to new situations. They then store that knowledge, effectively increasing their intelligence.

That all might sound pretty scary, but robots are still just tools designed for a specific purpose. They are unaware of their own existence and can only perform tasks for which they are programmed. They have no consciousness. It's possible to create programs that mimic thought, allowing a robot to recognize and respond to patterns, but it is still simply responding to commands, and the ability to give a robot consciousness—emotions and the free will to improve its own design—is beyond our grasp. It may be that consciousness can never be artificially simulated.

So if you live in constant fear of the day that humans become redundant and robots take over the world, you're okay—for now, anyway. But you might want to be a little nicer to your computer, just in case.

⇨ Is Red Wine Good for Your Health?

Given the amount of warnings we hear about the negative effects of drinking alcohol, it doesn't make sense that red wine would be good for you. And yet, that, too, is commonly heard. Is there any truth to this paradox, or is it a myth perpetuated by the wine manufacturers?

Oenophiles can rejoice: It's true. Red wine has a multitude of health benefits and drinking it could reduce a person's risk of heart attack, stroke, and cancer. It might also make you smarter and live longer. Sound too good to be true?

Studies have found that people who consume red wine have a 30 percent reduced risk of heart disease. Red wine contains antioxidants (in particular, resveratrol) that help prevent coronary artery disease by increasing the levels of high-density lipoprotein, the "good" cholesterol, thereby reducing "bad" cholesterol and blood clotting. Resveratrol comes from the skin of grapes, and because red wine is fermented with grape skins longer than white wine, red wine contains more of this beneficial substance. In fact, the darker the wine, the better.

Red wine also contains phenolic compounds that prevent the formation and growth of certain cancer cells. It has been found to reduce the risk of lung cancer and non-Hodgkin's lymphoma by between 20 and 40 percent, as well as bowel cancer by 20 percent.

Plus, red wine can make you smarter. Experts say it improves cognitive function, and may also reduce the risk of dementia. The resveratrol is also thought to protect against the effects of aging.

But, wine lovers, don't uncork a second bottle just yet. Red wine is only good for you in moderation. Any more than one or two glasses per day is likely to increase the chances of heart failure, stroke, high blood pressure, and certain types of cancer.

⇨ Do Bees Die After They Sting You?

A bee can only sting once, and when it does, it dies. Kids have been spouting this fact for decades, but is there any truth in it?

It depends on the type of bee. The stinger on a bee or wasp is a type of ovipositor (that is, an organ for depositing eggs). It is only female bees that sting; they inject venom into the victim through a stylus that is enclosed between a pair of lancets. When a bee or wasp stings you, the lancets become embedded in your skin.

In most bees and wasps, the lancets are fairly smooth, with only tiny barbs. After stinging, these barbs are easily retracted and the stinger can be removed.

However, in honeybees, the stinger is large, with backward-facing barbs on the lancets. When the worker honeybee stings you, these barbs dig into your flesh and lodge there, making it impossible for the bee to remove its stinger. As the bee tries to free the stinger and fly away, the stinger is torn from the bee's body, removing its abdomen and digestive tract, as well as some muscles and nerves. This abdominal rupture kills the bee.

The bee will only die if the skin of the animal it stings is sufficiently thick, preventing removal of the lancets and causing the abdominal rupture. So a honeybee would normally be able to sting an insect and live to sting again, but not a human.

So when a honeybee stings you, that is indeed the final act of its life. You may take some satisfaction in knowing that, but beware, as the bee often has the last laugh. In addition to the stinger, the bee's venom sacs are also left behind. If you squeeze the stinger to try to get it out, as many people do, it pumps even more poison into your body.

⇨ How Did the Term "Blackmail" Originate?

To blackmail is to extort money from someone, usually by the threat of exposing a damaging secret.

The word "blackmail" originated in the Scottish Highlands in the 17th century. The "mail" in the word comes from the Scottish *male*, meaning rent or tax. Farmers paid their usual rent in silver coins, which was known as white money, probably because of the light color of the silver. But farmers who lived along the remote Scottish-English border, away from the cities and larger towns, were subjected to a further tax.

The Highland clan chiefs set up a protection scheme. They threatened the locals with violence or theft of livestock if the farmers did not pay money to be protected from the other clans. This additional payment became known as black male, as opposed to the legitimate payment of white male.

By the 1900s, blackmail had developed the wider meaning that it has today.

⇨ Why Do Beans Make You Fart?

"Baked beans are good for your heart, baked beans make you fart." And so the catchy playground rhyme goes.

A can of baked beans is a good source of vegetable protein, as well as minerals such as potassium, magnesium, zinc, copper, calcium, and phosphorus. Beans are also low in fat, contain a number of vitamins, and are high in soluble fiber, which is beneficial for the digestive system. They're super quick and easy to prepare, as well. So, what's the catch?

They make you fart. Baked beans contain carbohydrates called oligosaccharides, a category that includes raffinose and stachyose. These carbohydrates give beans their natural

sweetness, but they are made of molecules that are too large for our small intestine to absorb during the digestion process. Instead, the molecules pass through to the lower intestine. It is the bacteria in that larger intestine that thrives on these molecules, breaking them down. As this metabolic process takes place, large amounts of gases are produced as a by-product, principally hydrogen, nitrogen, and carbon dioxide. These gases accumulate and escape the body as flatulence.

To reduce the amount of oligosaccharides in beans, they can be boiled and washed first. Another way to reduce gas is by taking an alpha-galactosidase supplement, such as Beano. The alpha-galactosidase enzyme breaks down the molecules, enabling them to be absorbed in the small intestine.

Failing that, just keep doing what you're doing and blame it on the dog.

⇨ Is Baldness in Men a Sign of Virility?

Have you ever found that when you mention a lack of hair to a bald man, he'll always reply, "It's a sign of virility"? The apparent link is testosterone. Bald men think that excess levels of testosterone lead to baldness, and as testosterone is the male hormone responsible for masculinity and sex drive, they are therefore more virile, as well.

The association of baldness with virility has been around for millennia. Hippocrates and Aristotle noticed the link between eunuchs (people who had been castrated) and their lack of hair loss. James B. Hamilton, an anatomy graduate from Yale University in the 1930s, also studied the topic, and noticed that men who had been castrated typically retained their hair.

While testosterone does cause baldness, it's not about the quantity circulating in the bloodstream, but rather how the testosterone signal is received in the hair follicle. And this comes down to genetics.

Male pattern balding is caused by an enzyme called 5-alpha reductase, which converts testosterone into dihydrotestosterone (DHT). DHT binds to receptor sites on the cells of hair follicles to cause specific changes. It inhibits hair growth, whereby healthy hair follicles start producing thinner and more brittle shafts of hair, and can even die out. Bald men are genetically predisposed to be more sensitive to DHT. It's not the amount of testosterone present that causes baldness; it's the fact that testosterone converts to DHT. Men with low levels of testosterone can go bald, as long as there is some testosterone.

But perhaps there's hope yet. Are bald men more virile anyway?

No. A balding British dermatologist named John Burton studied the correlation between baldness and virility in 1979. In his study of 48 men aged between 35 and 64, he found that typical markers of masculinity such as hair density on the body, testosterone levels, and muscle and bone thickness showed no relationship to baldness whatsoever. All later studies have come to the same conclusion.

This is bad news for the follically challenged men out there, but don't worry too much; you still have your beards. The chin follicles are not affected by DHT, so your beards will never fall out.

⇨ Why Does Paper Turn Yellow Over Time?

Paper is made from certain types of wood, and wood consists principally of two polymers: cellulose and lignin.

Cellulose is white, but lignin is a dark substance, and the lignin is what causes paper to turn yellow.

To make fine white paper, a paper mill puts the wood through a chemical solvent process that separates and removes the lignin. The chemical process adds to the expense, but paper that only contains cellulose will be white and will resist yellowing.

But with cheaper paper, such as that used for the bulk-printing, low-cost production of newspapers, the lignin is not removed.

Lignin has a naturally dark color and is what makes wood hard and stiff. When exposed to sunlight and oxygen in the air, the lignin molecules change and become less stable. The lignin undergoes oxidation and breaks down into phenolic acids that are yellow in color. The lignin also absorbs the light, giving off a darker color. As a result of these processes, within a fairly short space of time, the newspaper turns yellow. If it were kept completely out of the sun and air, it would remain white.

Paper manufacturers utilize the benefits of lignin when making cardboard and brown paper used for grocery store bags. The lignin in these types of papers makes them stiff and strong, and it's not as important for them to retain their original color.

⇨ Why Does Steam Come Up from the Streets of New York City?

If you watch a film and see steam coming up through the manholes and drain openings on the streets, you can be sure it's set in New York City. The steam is almost as well-known and iconic as the Empire State Building. But what is this steam, and where does it come from?

New York City relies on a power system that utilizes steam. Generating stations produce steam, which is then carried under the streets of Manhattan to heat, cool, and supply power to the buildings and businesses.

Started by the New York Steam Company in 1882, the system is now controlled by Con Edison, New York City's power company. They pipe steam to customers in Manhattan just

like any other utility product such as gas, electricity, or water. It is the largest steam system in the world, with around 24 billion pounds of steam flowing through it each year.

But why does the steam come up out of the streets, and is it dangerous?

The steam coming out is not steam from within the pipes; it's water vapor. When water, from rain or snow, falls through the manholes or down the street drains, it encounters the extremely hot steam pipes. When the water hits these pipes, it vaporizes and rises back up through the manholes as steam. The plumes tend to be bigger in winter when more external water falls into the manholes.

Sometimes the steam pipes do leak, and this is when large orange and white stacks are placed on the streets. They are used for the public's safety, ensuring the 350°F steam is pushed well above the street and away from people.

The system is very cost-effective in a densely populated setting. It is also energy efficient, reducing the usage of carbon fuel and pollution.

There are some dangers, however. Since 1987, at least 12 pipe explosions have occurred. In 1989, three people were killed, and an explosion in 2007 injured 40 people, killing one.

⇨ Where Did the Expression "Pay Through the Nose" Originate?

"To pay through the nose" means to pay an excessive amount for something. For example, if you just bought the best car on the market, you might say, "The performance of the car is even better than I expected, but I did pay through the nose for it." How did this strange expression originate?

The phrase dates all the way back to the 9th century, when the Vikings from Denmark invaded Ireland.

The Danish had extraordinarily harsh tax laws, which they imposed on any land they invaded. With the invasion of Ireland, they applied a particularly high tax known as the Nose Tax. The punishment for evading the Nose Tax was draconian and perverse. Anyone refusing to pay the tax had their nose slit from tip to eyebrow.

The people had a choice: Either pay the tax, or pay through the nose. No contest.

⇨ Why Do Police Officers Hold Flashlights with an Overhand Grip?

In any cop movie or television show, the police officers always hold their flashlights in an overhand, or ice pick, grip. Nobody else ever seems to hold flashlights in this way, so why do the police?

The main reason is that by holding the light in this position, it can more easily be used as a defensive weapon. In the dark, an attack on the officer is likely to be unexpected, so the metal flashlight can be used to strike down on an attacker with force. If it were carried the other way, it would have to be raised and then lowered to hit someone. This would take up valuable time.

Holding it in this way can also act as a defensive device. With the light up high and away from the body, the idea is that the officer will disorient any attacker, who will tend to shoot at the light and miss the officer's body. Most people also tend to shoot high of a target; when they pull the trigger they jerk it, and the gun lifts, as well. This makes it more likely that any bullet would pass over the officer. If the light were held down low, the officer's body would be directly behind the light source and would be more likely to be hit by a bullet.

It is also more effective if an officer is looking into a car. With an underhanded grip, the officer would have to bend down to see. With an overhanded grip, it is far less awkward.

Another major advantage of the ice pick grip is that when cops in the movies hold a flashlight that way, it looks cool. And real-life police officers watch cop shows just like the rest of us.

⇨ How Do Figure Skaters Keep from Getting Dizzy?

Figure skaters are known for their dazzlingly fast turns and for captivating audiences by spinning around and around in one place at lightning speed. Given that most people get dizzy after only a few spins on normal ground, why don't they?

Dancers avoid dizziness when pirouetting by keeping their eyes locked on a fixed point, and then whipping their heads around when their necks can't turn any more. This means that while the rest of their body is spinning, their eyes trick the brain into thinking they're standing still. This vastly reduces any dizziness they suffer. But ice skaters spin much too fast to make that technique either safe or possible.

Given that the ice is slippery and any mistake can be disastrous, they do other things to combat dizziness. They do try to keep their eyes horizontal so their view only spins around one axis, and they also try to maintain a constant pace to their spins. The sensors in the ear's vestibular system, where dizziness occurs, can only detect changes in speed, so if a skater can keep a constant speed when rotating, the effects of dizziness will only be encountered when they accelerate into or slow down out of a spin.

But the main dizziness-combatting weapon of the skater is practice. Skaters do get dizzy, but a lot of training means that they are able to ignore it because they're used to it. They also gradually build up to the spins when practicing as a beginner. They start with only a few rotations, getting used to the associated dizziness before attempting more complicated moves. After years of practice, they are able to ignore the sensation

of dizziness and carry on as normal, without it upsetting their routine.

Skaters have a couple of other tricks, as well. They use breathing exercises to help regain their control after spinning, and they also often incorporate a dance move into their routine after a long spin. They do this before going into a difficult jump, as it masks their dizziness and gives them time to adjust back to normal.

So, the next time you're watching the figure skating at the Winter Olympics, bear in mind that just because the skaters are smiling, it doesn't mean that they don't feel like they're about to throw up.

⇨ What Do Women Look For in a Man?

It is the question that every man since Plato has wanted the answer to: What do women look for in a man?

There are numerous qualities in men that women generally cite as being attractive. Here are a few:

- has good grooming and dress sense (women hate a slob)
- has a good physique (indicating health and the ability to produce strong offspring)
- is not a pushover (women like a challenge)
- has confidence (demonstrates the ability to meet challenges and face adversities)
- is assertive yet charming
- is respected by others
- is respectful (women see kind men as good fathers)
- is a good listener (women like to talk)
- has a good job and salary (for obvious reasons)

But above all of these factors, studies have shown that there are two other things that every woman wants.

If you ask 100 women what they look for in a man, 99 will respond with "someone who can make me laugh." In his 2011 study, Gil Greengross, a psychologist and anthropologist from the University of Mexico, found that humor is very important to women when selecting a mate. It makes women assume the man is smarter, as the ability to say something funny requires a higher level of intelligence. Humor is one of the top traits that consistently shows up in surveys of women's preferences, and men who are funny are reported to have a more active sex life than other men.

But there's something even higher on the scale than humor. Most studies show that altruism is the top quality that women are drawn to when looking for a man. A number of studies in the last decade have found that generous men had more relationships and more sex than stingy men. One 2013 study found that women valued altruism above all other traits as a measure of whether a man would make a good father. In another study from 2015, single men who did good deeds were more likely to find a partner and typically found one faster than other men did.

To back this up, in a 2016 study published in the *British Journal of Psychology*, researchers found that altruistic men generally had more sex. Subjects who said they gave money to charity or did good deeds were reported to have more sex and more partners. In the second experiment of the study, a group of college students were asked if they'd like to donate the money they received for participating in the study to charity. Those who said they would were reported as having more casual sex, more sex in relationships, and more partners over their life.

But there's hope yet for the selfish men out there. Most studies have found that women were particularly interested in altruism when it came to finding a long-term partner. In a 2016 study published in a journal called *Evolutionary Psychology*, women searching for a long-term relationship were inclined to choose an altruistic man no matter what he looked like. But when it came to a one-night stand, the women chose the physically attractive men, whether they were selfish or not.

So, it turns out that the lyrics from that Good Charlotte song "Girls & Boys" aren't quite right after all. Girls like cars and money, and funny, intelligent men who are willing to give those cars away to strangers. But if you're a man just looking for a one-night stand, you might as well keep your belongings.

⇨ Why Was 911 Chosen as the Emergency Number?

The best-known phone number in the world is probably 911. It is the emergency number throughout the United States, and is known in many other countries who broadcast the television show *Rescue 911*.

But were those numbers just picked at random, or was there some logic to them?

Before the 1960s, the United States didn't have a single universal emergency phone number. People had to call different numbers for each emergency department in their local area. This made things very confusing. With thousands of numbers being used across America, each household had to know lengthy numbers for reaching firefighters, police, or ambulances.

Then in 1957, the National Association of Fire Chiefs recommended the use of a single phone number for reporting fires. But it wasn't until 1967 that various government agencies supported this idea and directed the Federal Communications Commission to come up with a solution.

The FCC met with AT&T to find a universal emergency number that could be implemented without much delay. In 1968, AT&T announced that 911 would be that emergency number. But why 911?

The number was chosen for a variety of reasons. Most importantly, it was short and could be dialed quickly using the old-style rotary phones, which still existed at the time. And being so brief, it was easy to remember. Another key factor was that it was unique and had never been used as a code in America before—not an office code, an area code, or a service code.

It could also be easily distinguished from other, longer phone numbers in AT&T's internal system, which meant it could be routed to a special location with minimal changes to the AT&T network.

The first 911 call was made on February 16, 1968, by Senator Rankin Fite in Haleyville, Alabama. Now, an estimated

240 million calls are made to the number each year in the United States.

⇨ Why Is the Clink Slang for Jail?

"The clink" is a slang or informal term for jail. When you hear that someone has been sent to the clink, it means they have gone to prison. Where did this term originate?

Some believe that the term comes from the clinking sound of metal jail doors being shut, or a key in a metal lock. But it actually derives from a notorious prison of that name in Southwark, London.

The Clink functioned as a prison from the 13th century until 1780, and it is thought to be the oldest prison in England. The Liberty of Clink was the name of the district in which the prison was located, which was south of the River Thames and outside the jurisdiction of the City of London. As a consequence, the Clink set its own rules and was known for its extreme punishments, including the rack, the wheel, and boiling in oil.

The Clink was burnt down by rioters in 1780, and the location is now home to a museum, built on the original site.

⇨ Do Carrots Really Help Eyesight?

Parents will say anything to get their kids to eat vegetables. "Eat all your carrots and you'll have good eyesight," is one line that is commonly heard at the dinner table. Many children must wonder if there's any truth to what they're being told.

This carrot-eyesight adage actually stems from World War II. The UK Ministry of Food at the time reported that eating carrots was the key to the pilots' success over the Germans, saying the carrots gave them enhanced night  vision. It was later suggested that the British Royal Air Force had pushed that message to cover up the fact that they were actually using improved radar technology.

So, that's how it all started, but is there any scientific basis to it?

Carrots are beneficial for overall vision health. They are rich in beta-carotene, a carotenoid pigment that the body converts into vitamin A. Vitamin A helps convert light into a signal that can be transmitted to the brain, and can prevent the formation of cataracts and macular degeneration. Deficiencies in vitamin A are the leading cause of blindness in the developing world, where supplements have been shown to improve vision. It is an essential nutrient for eye health.

Carrots also contain lutein, which is an important antioxidant. Lutein increases the density of pigment in the macula, the oval-shaped yellow area in the center of the retina. This protects the retina and reduces the risk of macular degeneration diseases.

That said, other foods contain these ingredients. Spinach, kale, and leafy greens also contain lutein. And fortified rice, goat liver, and amaranth leaf contain vitamin A. In a study conducted in 2005, it was found that all these vitamin A-rich foods performed the same as carrots when it came to helping night blindness in pregnant women, but vitamin A supplements were far more effective.

The question remains as to whether carrots will improve your vision. Yes and no, is the answer. If your vision is already impaired, carrots are very unlikely to improve it, but they do promote overall eye health.

This means that parents can tell their children that carrots are good for their eyes with a clear conscience, but don't expect them to lose their glasses just because they eat their carrots.

⇨ Why Are Pigs Roasted with an Apple in the Mouth?

The tradition of putting an apple in a roasting pig's mouth has existed for over 800 years. It has been done for centuries in many areas of the world, including Asia, Europe, the Middle East, the Caribbean, and Polynesia. Roasting pork is still popular today, with many Europeans doing it as a celebration for Christmas, while Asians cook it to mark the New Year. And still, the apple is put in the hog's mouth. Why?

Some people claim that the apple is used to keep the pig's mouth open to allow toxic gases to be released while the pig roasts. This is incorrect. The main internal organs of the pig are removed before it is cooked, so no toxic gases are produced that need to escape.

The real answer is actually pretty simple. It's for aesthetics. The snout of a pig is not very nice to look at, and the cooking process makes it worse by tightening the pig's jaws and giving it a snarling appearance. The apple softens this look and makes the head of the pig more visually appealing.

It is believed by some that the apple was specifically chosen because of how pigs were raised hundreds of years ago. To prepare them for eating, pigs were fattened with apples, so putting the fruit in the pig's mouth before roasting was a way of representing the full circle of life—the pig would be eating the apple in both life and death.

⇨ Why Didn't People Smile in Old Photos?

Historical accounts say that Charles Darwin was very friendly, Abraham Lincoln had a humorous persona, and Mark Twain was armed with a sharp wit. But anybody looking at photographs of these three would assume they were the most serious and gloomy men who ever lived. In the photos of today, people smile and laugh, desperate to show how happy and social they are. Why did our ancestors appear so disconsolate when being photographed?

Some claim that people of yesteryear froze in their photos to allow for the longer exposure times in the cameras, or that they didn't want to show off their rotting teeth. Both of these suggestions are unlikely. And while times were often financially harder when photography began, it's not as if laughter and mirth did not exist—carnivals and court jesters were the order of the day, so people loved to have a good time.

The reasons lie in the attitudes to both smiling and portraiture that existed in that era.

While today we think of smiles as being an indication of humor and happiness, in the 1800s it was believed that people who smiled a lot were poor, drunk, or simple. Those of higher standing and character did not readily smile in public.

In addition to that, it was traditional for people not to smile when having their portrait painted. In the early days of photography, having a photograph taken was not dissimilar to having a portrait done—it was a rare occurrence, and for many people, it was a once-in-a-lifetime experience. People understood being photographed as a significant moment, intended as a timeless record of a person, much like a portrait was. Technology had given people the chance to be "painted" like a king, and they took it very seriously. As Mark Twain once wrote, "A photograph is a most important document, and

there is nothing more damning to go down to posterity than a silly, foolish smile caught and fixed forever."

The question then becomes, why did we start smiling in photos?

By the early 1900s, in an attempt to associate their products with happiness and good times, companies used pictures of smiling models in their marketing campaigns. Kodak was no exception. They advertised heavily with smiling models, emphasizing the pleasure of the photograph. People soon began smiling in photos and the trend continued to modern times.

⇨ What's the Origin of the "Six Degrees of Separation" Theory?

Six degrees of separation is the theory that every person in the world can be connected to any other person through a chain of no more than five other people. It does seem a little far-fetched that the Queen of England knows someone, who knows someone, and the person only three later knows a child who's living in a mud hut in Africa. What are the chances?

Actually, very high.

The theory was first proposed in 1929 by the Hungarian writer Frigyes Karinthy in a short story called *Chains*. Then, in the 1950s, Ithiel de Sola Pool from MIT and Manfred Kochen from IBM set out to prove it mathematically. They were unable to fully prove the theory, and it wasn't until 1967, with an experiment devised by the American sociologist Stanley Milgram, that it was properly put to the test. Milgram randomly selected people in the Midwest to send packages to different strangers in Massachusetts. The people knew the recipient's name, occupation, and general location. They were instructed to send the package to anyone they knew personally, who they believed was the most likely to know the recipient. The person they sent it to would do the same, and so on, until the package was delivered. Most people expected the chain to include hundreds of people, but on average, it took only five to seven intermediaries for each package to be successfully delivered.

Milgram's findings, entitled "The Small World Problem," were published in *Psychology Today*, a popular science journal. The article generated enormous publicity for the experiments and inspired the phrase "six degrees of separation," although the playwright John Guare popularized the phrase when he chose it as the title for his 1990 play.

In 2001, Duncan Watts, a professor at Columbia University, tested Milgram's theory on the Internet, using an e-mail as the "package" to be delivered. After reviewing the data collected across 157 countries by 48,000 senders and 19 recipients, Watts discovered that the average number of intermediaries was indeed six.

It is unlikely that Stanley Milgram knew what sort of impact his experiment was going to have on today's culture when he started it in 1967. He was probably also not thinking about a nine-year-old Pennsylvanian boy who would later inspire so many discussions on the point that a game was developed in his honor—Six Degrees of Kevin Bacon.

⇨ Why Are Male Birds More Colorful Than Female Birds?

In the vast majority of bird species, the male parades around looking regal with brightly colored plumage, while the female is dull and drab. It hardly seems fair, but there is a scientific explanation for this ornithological phenomenon.

Charles Darwin developed much of the theory that explains the differences in birds. He proposed that in animals where the males must compete for mates, certain characteristics that are unique to the males are propagated because of sexual selection. These features are either weapons that allow the males to fight for the females, such as the horns on a buffalo, or ornaments that attract the attention of the females, such as colorful feathers in birds.

Female birds see the brightness of the male as an important indicator of his health. A colorful male is a strong and healthy one, better able to acquire plentiful food for them both, as well as for any chicks. This has been proven in a number of instances. In the house finch, the brightness of the male is directly related to the pigments obtained from high-quality seed. Brighter birds of other species have also been shown to be better at providing food for females than their duller counterparts.

Color in male birds is also used as a defense when fighting other males for territory. As color indicates health and strength, a brightly colored male is more likely to scare his opponents away. With the red-winged black bird, scientists have found that when the male's wings are artificially dyed completely black, the bird is more likely to lose his territory.

Female birds are usually dull for a reason, too. When nesting, they are more at risk of being attacked by predators, so a bland appearance allows them to blend in with their surroundings.

However, where gender roles are reversed and the male incubates the eggs while the female defends the territory and fights for access to the males, the female bird has the more colorful plumage. Sandpipers, phalaropes, and button quail are examples of this.

⇨ Why Don't You Get Goose Bumps on Your Face?

Everyone gets goose bumps from time to time. The last time you heard the "National Anthem" playing, you might have gotten them all over your arms and legs—but not on your face.

Goose bumps form when a person is cold, apprehensive, excited, or afraid. They are caused by a reflex called piloerection, which occurs when the muscles at the base of each hair follicle (known as the arrector pili muscles) contract and pull the hair erect. The piloerection reflex is governed by the sympathetic nervous system, which is responsible for the fight-or-flight response in animals. Once a particular stimulus exists, nerves discharge, causing the muscles to contract and the hairs to stand. This makes an animal look bigger and more imposing. They also insulate animals against the cold because a layer of air gets trapped under the hairs. In humans, the same phenomenon occurs, except that our hair is not thick enough to be obvious when it stands up. Each contracting muscle, however, creates a shallow depression on the skin, causing the area surrounding the hair follicle to protrude. The effect is goose bumps.

Several parts of the body do not have arrector pili muscles. These are areas where the skin serves a specific purpose, such as how the skin on our palms assists with grasping objects. Arrector pili muscles do exist on the face, but they have developed to be used for facial expressions rather than controlling hair follicles. In most animals, including humans, these muscles in the face assist with chewing and keeping the mouth closed, but they also allow us to smile, frown, grimace, and make a multitude of other expressions to convey emotion. It is because of these other, more important muscular functions that we don't get goose bumps on our faces.

▷ How Do Cats See in the Dark?

It is well-known that cats have excellent night vision, which adapted to allow them to hunt effectively in the dark. There is, of course, a physiological basis for this.

The main difference between human vision and cat vision is the retina, a layer of tissue at the rear of the eye that contains cells called photoreceptors. These cells convert light into electrical signals, which are then processed by nerve cells, sent to the brain, and translated into images.

There are two types of photoreceptor cells: rods and cones. Rods are responsible for peripheral and night vision. Cats have a high concentration of rods, up to eight times as many as humans have. These additional rods also give cats a wider field of vision—about 200 degrees, compared with 180 degrees for humans.

Cats also have a structure behind the retina called the tapetum lucidum, which improves night vision. Cells in it act like a mirror, reflecting light back to the photoreceptors to give them every possible chance to detect all available light at night. It is the tapetum lucidum that makes cats' eyes glow in the dark. Cats also have an elliptical eye shape and a larger cornea that helps take in more light.

All of these factors give cats night vision, which is seven times better than that of humans.

However, cats have fewer cones, the other photoreceptor cells. Cones are responsible for day vision and color perception. Humans have more cones than cats, meaning we can detect colors better. It also means that cats are sensitive to excess light, causing the slit-like pupil to close narrowly over the eye in bright conditions.

What does all this mean? If you come face to face with a lion, you'd better hope you're in a blindingly bright room, wearing a very colorful shirt, and standing at an extremely obtuse angle.

⇨ What Is MSG, and Why Do Only Chinese Restaurants Use It?

Monosodium glutamate, or MSG, is the sodium salt of glutamic acid. It is found naturally in certain foods, including cheese and tomatoes. MSG is used in the food industry as a flavor enhancer, intensifying the savory taste of food. It was first prepared as a seasoning in 1908 by a Japanese biochemist named Kikunae Ikeda.

MSG is surrounded by controversy, with some people claiming that it allows the use of lower quality or less fresh ingredients without compromising on flavor. It is widely known for its heavy use in Chinese food, which led to "Chinese restaurant syndrome," a term coined in the 1960s. The syndrome relates to the symptoms that some people say they experience after eating the food, including headaches, sweating, and flushing of the skin.

There is, however, minimal scientific evidence supporting a link between MSG and the symptoms of the syndrome, and a number of studies have failed to show any association. The US Food and Drug Administration has given MSG a GRAS designation (generally recognized as safe). Nevertheless, the negative public perception surrounding MSG has led many restaurants to stop using it, and they usually advertise that fact strongly.

But why is it only Chinese restaurants that use MSG?

It's not. Many people associate MSG with Chinese food because it is used so extensively throughout China and Chinese restaurants abroad. But, in reality, it is used in many other restaurants, particularly in the fast food industry. KFC, Burger King, Pizza Hut, and many others all flavor some of their items with MSG; they're just not as well-known for it.

⇨ Why Can't We Remember Our Early Childhood?

Most people suffer from a condition known as childhood amnesia, in which the memories from early childhood are either nonexistent or very hazy. Quite often, they don't exist, but we construct them from photos or stories told to us. While nearly everyone experiences this phenomenon, it still puzzles psychologists, and the explanation for it is not clear. There are four hypotheses, and most scientists agree that one, or a combination of them, is the likely cause.

1. An Underdeveloped Brain. The infant brain isn't developed enough to form long-term memories. The hippocampus, which is the part of the brain responsible for forming memories, is fairly developed by the age of one, but continues developing until at least the age of seven. The prefrontal cortex, which scientists believe helps us to form episodic memories, also doesn't fully mature until our early twenties. While we might remember skills or particular items, we can't remember actual events. In one study, six-month-olds who learned to press a lever to operate a train remembered how to do it for three weeks after they had last seen the toy. However, they couldn't remember events that happened to them.

2. Limited Language Skills. Some experts believe that infants can't remember because they can't frame memories in linguistic terms, which prevents the memories from being organized and stored properly. While we don't need language to form memories, it helps us to rehearse them, both aloud to other people and in our heads. The suggestion is that the memories are formed, but can't be maintained. One study interviewed people who had been to the hospital for an injury when they were toddlers. The infants aged over 26 months, who were able to speak at the time, remembered the incident up to five years later, while those under 26 months, who could not talk at the time, recalled nothing.

3. No Sense of Self. Some believe that infants need to develop a sense of self before they can remember things that happened to them. In one study, infants who could recognize themselves in a mirror had far better memory recall of where they'd hidden a teddy bear than those who could not.

4. No Retrieval Cues. Some experts think that infants have no trouble forming memories; they just can't recall them later in life. The theory is that because our perspective has changed so much since our early childhood, there are no retrieval cues to trigger a memory. They claim that even if we live in the same house, everything looks so much different when we're older that nothing cues the memory. For example, a chair that once looked enormous later seems much smaller.

Despite the lack of memories that infants may have, it is universally accepted by psychologists that the accumulation of events does nevertheless have a lasting and powerful influence in shaping their personalities as adults.

▷ Why Do Bicycle Tires Go Flat If a Bike Is Not Used for a Long Time?

Has anyone ever noticed that you can ride your bike every day for a month and never need to pump the tires up, but after not riding it for a week, the tires have gone flat? It doesn't seem to make any sense, but here's why it happens.

The rubber that comprises the tire tube is slightly permeable, so all tires will leak a certain amount of air. However, when a bike is ridden, the pressure in the tires remains high because the heat that is generated from motion expands the air they contain. This pressure helps to seal the tire against the rim of the wheel. But when a bike is not ridden for a while, the pressure in the tires reduces, and the tire is not pushed as tightly against the rim. This allows more air to escape between the tire and the rim.

When a bike sits for a long time, the tires can also experience what's called flatspotting, which is where the tire develops a flat area where it's touching the ground. When a tire is cold and remains in one place without moving, the rubber distorts in the area that's touching the ground because all the weight is pressed into one place instead of being evenly distributed across a moving tire. This also means that the tire is pushed unevenly against the rim, allowing air to escape from certain places. Bicycles not in use should be hung up to avoid flatspotting.

Despite all of this, here's the real reason that tires deflate: The bike is protesting because you've neglected it.

⇨ When Did Humans Discover That the Earth Is Round?

For many years, humans believed that the earth was flat. In all parts of the civilized world, including Europe, Asia, and China, the people viewed the earth as a plane or disk. The early Egyptians and Mesopotamians saw the world as a flat disk floating in the ocean.

The discovery that the earth is spherical is credited to the Greek philosopher Pythagoras. He theorized in the 6th century BC that the earth was not flat, but was a spherical body in orbit around the sun.

Then, the great Greek philosopher Aristotle proved it. In around 330 BC, he demonstrated that the earth was a sphere by explaining the curvature of the horizon and the way a ship disappears over it.

The first person to definitively prove this in practice was the Portuguese explorer Ferdinand Magellan. When he circumnavigated the globe in 1522, dying just before reaching the end, the case was closed.

A popular myth exists that when he sailed from Spain across the Atlantic in 1492, Christopher Columbus was the first person to disprove the common belief that the earth was flat. This is incorrect, and there was no debate over the earth's shape before his voyage. It had been accepted since the time of the ancient Greeks that the earth was round, and Columbus would have certainly held that belief without question. The myth is thought to have originated with Washington Irving's 1828 biography *The Life and Voyages of Christopher Columbus*. In it, he wrote that Columbus's voyages to the New World proved that the earth was round.

⇨ Why Is There Sometimes Sand in the Pockets of New Blue Jeans?

Often after putting on your new blue jeans, you'll put your hands in the pockets and find that there's sand in there. How can this be? Have they been test-driven by the manufacturer or worn by the sales assistant at the beach? No. They've been sandblasted.

Many consumers are willing to pay extra for jeans that have the appearance of being used—for some reason, people love the worn look. This fashion trend developed in the 1990s and continues today.

To give jeans that distressed look, manufacturers use a technique called sandblasting. Sandblasting is a way of speeding up the process of wear and tear. Workers shoot abrasive sand onto the denim jeans. The fine sand is channeled into an air gun then sprayed at high pressure at the jeans. It is a fast, cheap way of making the jeans appear much older than they really are. But even after the jeans are later washed, some sand will often remain in the pockets.

This sandblasting technique has caused great controversy in the industry. It is generally done in bad conditions, where ventilation is poor and little safety equipment is used. In 2004, a Turkish doctor established a link between former denim plant workers and silicosis, a fatal lung disease caused by inhaling tiny pieces of silica, a mineral found in sand. Turkey is a major clothing manufacturing country, and its government banned the practice in 2009. A further study confirmed that silicosis is highly likely among sandblasters.

By 2010, 40 major denim brands, including Levi-Strauss & Co., H&M, Armani, and Versace, had banned sandblasting on their jeans. However, many believe that the practice is still used in some countries, particularly parts of North Africa and in China.

Distressed jeans have certainly caused some serious distress in the denim industry, and as a result, there is now a far less likely chance that the pockets of your new jeans will feel like they've just had a day at the beach.

▷ Why Does Ice Cream Give You Brain Freeze?

Most children love ice cream. So much so, their enthusiasm for it often makes them eat it way too quickly. A few seconds later, and bang, brain freeze hits.

Also known as an ice cream headache, brain freeze is the sharp pain that a person experiences in their head after eating something cold. It usually lasts between 10 and 30 seconds.

The prevailing causal theory is that when something cold touches the roof of your mouth, one of the nerves in that area, the trigeminal nerve, responds by dilating blood vessels in the head. It does this in an effort to increase blood flow to the brain to keep it warm. This rapid swelling of the blood vessels creates a pulsating headache.

Other experts believe that while the trigeminal nerve is responsible for a brain freeze, it causes the reaction by referring the pain. Instead of feeling the sensation on the roof of the mouth, the pain is transferred along the nerve pathway to the head, where a headache results.

The best way to avoid a brain freeze is to eat ice cream slowly. But if you do get one and don't want to finish the rest, whatever you do, don't give it to your cat. They get brain freezes, too.

⇨ Does Alcohol Really Kill Brain Cells?

How many times do you hear it: "Don't drink too much alcohol, it'll kill your brain cells"? There is clear evidence that alcohol does do something to the brain. After a few drinks, people will slur their words, stumble when they walk, and experience memory loss. But have brain cells actually been killed, or is there another way to explain these debilitating symptoms?

Alcohol does not kill brain cells, but it does affect the brain. When it reaches the brain, alcohol inhibits the dendrites, the branching connections at the ends of neurons that send and receive messages between brain cells. This results in poor communication between the cells, causing cognitive and motor problems.

However, the brain has billions of neurons and dendrites, and research has shown that dendrite damage is reversible. Even in alcoholics, once drinking is stopped for a period of time, the dendrites repair and the ability of the brain cells to communicate is restored. Most significant, long-term

alcohol-related disabilities are actually caused by malnutrition or a deficiency in vitamins.

Another side effect of excessive drinking is that alcohol inhibits the growth of new brain cells. But research on rats has shown that once the alcohol intake is stopped, even more brain cells are produced to compensate.

So, while alcohol can impair your brain, the effects are generally temporary and reversible. In fact, a number of studies have shown that drinking moderate amounts actually improves brain function and is associated with a reduced risk of dementia. It has been found that those who drink moderately on a regular basis have a reduced chance of becoming mentally ill later in life compared to those who don't drink. One study from 2001, conducted at the Catholic University of the Sacred Heart in Italy, found there was a 19 percent chance of mental impairment for people over 65 who were drinkers, as opposed to a 29 percent chance in non-drinkers.

⇨ Why Are Old Men Sexually Reproductive but Old Women Aren't?

Clint Eastwood had a child when he was 66, and the oldest man to have a child is thought to be an Indian aged 96. There are numerous examples of men having children late in life, whereas even the early 40s is considered old for women.

A man's sperm production continues throughout his life, while a woman is born with all the eggs she will ever have. By the time a woman is 30 years old, 90 percent of her eggs are gone, and by 40, only three percent are left. It is the evolutionary goal of any organism to pass on its genes, so scientists are not exactly sure why women have such a long post-reproductive life. No other primate is like that, so why are we?

One theory is that the women of our early ancestors did not live long lives, so they would have been able to have children until their death. Because of modern medicine, women now live longer, but the timing of menopause has not changed.

Another theory is that mothers need to be young and strong so that they are better able to care for their children. Infants require an extended period of intense care, unable to fend for themselves for years, so a mother needs to be capable. Men, on the other hand, don't necessarily have a role after insemination, so this doesn't apply to them, and they are left to reproduce into old age.

Others claim that humans developed this strategy to avoid competition between generations of women in one family. If a mother and her daughter were pregnant at the same time under the same roof, the resources would need to be split between competing infants, reducing both of their chances of survival.

Probably the most popular hypothesis, however, is the grandmother hypothesis. This states that menopause allows older women to use their resources to help raise their grandchildren. The older women are not exposed to the risks associated with childbirth, and are thus more likely to live longer and help raise the infants to adulthood. One study found that children are 12 percent more likely to survive to adulthood when they have the support of a grandmother.

A team at McMaster University in Ontario came up with a more controversial theory in 2013 to explain menopause in women. They suggested that our ancestral men had a strong preference for mating with younger women, which left older women without mates. The women then evolved so that they were unable to reproduce past a certain age. Critics of this say it is purely theoretical, without any practical facts.

It is unlikely that scientists will ever know the exact reason for early menopause in women; it is most probably a combination of these factors.

⇨ Why Do Beavers Build Dams?

The beaver dam requires an incredible amount of work. The beavers have to chew through tree trunks, then carry the timber between their teeth and mud and stones with their paws. They start by diverting a stream with logs to reduce the flow of the water, before driving branches and logs into the stream bed to form a base. Sticks, rocks, mud, grass, leaves, bark, and plants are then used to build the main body of the structure. The average dam is 5.9 feet high, 3 feet thick, and

14 feet long, and it creates a large flooded area known as a beaver pond. Why would any animal go to so much trouble?

The answer is simple: food and safety.

Beavers are herbivores and prefer the wood of various trees, including the birch, maple, and cherry trees. They also eat weeds and water lilies. By creating a dam that is filled with this material, they have access to an abundant source of food without needing to travel across land, which would risk an attack by predators.

The other purpose of the beaver pond is to keep beavers safe from predators such as wolves, bears, and coyotes. The pond is usually about five feet deep, which affords them adequate protection. Beavers don't actually live in the dams they've built. They live in lodges that they build in the deep dam ponds with the same materials used for the dam. They cover the lodges with mud, which freezes in the winter, making them impenetrable to predators. The beavers use underwater entrances, which makes entry to the lodge virtually impossible for other animals.

⇨ Why Do Women Open Their Mouths When Applying Mascara?

If you're a woman who's applied mascara, or a man who's watched it being applied, you've probably wondered the same thing: Why on earth do women open their mouths while doing it?

There are a number of theories as to why this peculiar phenomenon occurs.

- Keeping your mouth shut requires effort. When you're relaxed or concentrating on a delicate task, the neck muscles slacken and the mouth opens spontaneously. Many women don't even know it's happening.

- Having the mouth open in an "O" shape temporarily stops a person from blinking, which is preferable when applying mascara.

- The mouth muscles are used to help move the facial muscles in order to get at the different lashes, particularly the more difficult corner lashes.

- When the mouth is opened, the eyes naturally open wider, making it easier to apply the mascara.

- Opening the mouth stretches out the skin around the eyes. This helps to keep the skin farther away from the lashes so the mascara doesn't smudge on the skin.

- It is an unconscious and involuntary response that occurs when someone is concentrating, similar to how people sometimes stick out their tongues when doing another task.

- There is no reason at all. Women are strange and will never be fully understood.

Now, go on to the next question, and stop moving your mouth around to test these theories.

⇨ Why Does an "X" Stand for a Kiss and an "O" for a Hug?

Known as hugs and kisses, XOXO is often placed at the end of a message in a letter, e-mail, or text to express love, sincerity, or friendship.

Signing a letter or document with an "X" dates back to medieval times. During that period, many people couldn't read or write, so an "X" was often used as a simple way for someone to sign a legal document. Placing an "X" at the end of a document was a means of saying that whatever was in the document was true. The letter "X" represented Jesus Christ, so that by signing "X", the person was asserting, "In Christ's name, it's true."

The letter "X" had been used as a substitute for Christ since about 1,000 AD, which is how Xmas was derived as an alternative name for Christmas. The "X" is not supposed to replicate the shape of Christ's cross, and is not the English "X." It is actually the Greek letter "Chi," which is an "X," the first letter in the Greek word for Christ.

Historians believe that the "X" then came to symbolize a kiss because of the practice of people kissing it on the page, the same way some would kiss the Bible. The "X" would be written and then "sealed with a kiss." "X" has represented a kiss in this way since the mid-1700s.

How the letter "O" came to mean a hug is less certain. The most popular theory is that it began in the United States with illiterate Jewish immigrants. Unable to sign their name, and refusing to sign with an "X" because they rejected the notion of Jesus as God, they signed with a circle instead.

Perhaps because the shape of an "O" is similar to encircling arms, it came to represent a hug.

⇨ Why Do Boxers Make a Sniffing Noise When They Throw Punches?

Every time a professional boxer throws a punch, he makes a sniffing sound. Is there any point to this, or is it just done for effect?

Known in boxing circles as the snort, this is the sound of the boxer breathing out sharply. A boxer must regulate his breathing or he will quickly tire. Holding the breath while punching causes fatigue, so it is important for a boxer to develop a breathing rhythm. Each time he throws a punch, the boxer will exhale, and after a combination, he will breathe back in.

In addition to the exhaling breath being done sharply, there is another reason why it makes such a snorting noise: It is done through the nose. Boxers are taught to keep their mouths tightly closed when in close contact to their opponent so that if they are hit in the jaw, the impact will cause less damage.

Some boxers claim that the snort also gives the punch extra power. Many dispute this, but there is some logic to it. When a boxer is about to punch an opponent, he contracts his muscles. Exhaling tightens his core further, adding more force to the punch.

Others claim that the snort has no point at all, but boxers merely do it because everyone else does. Whether this is true or not, the snort is here to stay. If nothing else, it makes boxers seem a lot more intimidating.

⇨ How Did Mumbo Jumbo Come to Mean Unintelligible Talk?

Mumbo jumbo means nonsense, or meaningless, unintelligible, or complicated speech or writing. It is often used to refer to overly technical documents, such as "legal mumbo jumbo."

The expression originated with the early explorers of Africa in the 18th century. Francis Moore was one of the first Englishmen to travel into the interior of the continent, and in 1738, he wrote the book *Travels into the Inland Parts of Africa*. In his book, he describes how the men of one tribe, the Mundingoes, employed the assistance of a legendary spirit who would scream nonsensical ramblings to ensure obedience in their women.

"The women are kept in the greatest subjection," he wrote, "and the men, to render their power as complete as possible, influence their wives to give them an unlimited obedience, by all the force of fear and terror. For this purpose, the Mundingoes have a kind of image eight or nine feet high, made of the bark of trees, dressed in a long coat, and crowned with a wisp of straw. This is called a Mumbo Jumbo; and whenever the men have any dispute with the women, this is sent for to determine the contest, which is almost always done in favor of the men."

It was this passage that brought the term "mumbo jumbo" to the masses, and by the mid-1800s, the phrase had come to mean any meaningless ranting.

⇨ Why Don't Penguins Get Frostbite on Their Feet?

Imagine not only living in freezing temperatures, but being made to stand outside in the frigid wind, directly on the ice, barefoot. Welcome to the world of the penguin. Humans wouldn't last 10 minutes before their feet were frostbitten and useless. How do penguins do it?

Penguins have adapted to avoid losing too much heat in order to preserve their body temperature. Their feet pose a problem, however, as they are not insulated by thick, downy feathers. But penguins have evolved to handle this, as well.

Their feet and lower legs consist mainly of bone, tendons, and a thick layer of skin, but the muscles used to control the feet are higher up on the leg and are covered by warm feathers and fat. This warmth allows the foot muscles to function properly.

The penguin has also adapted so that its feet are kept just above the freezing point. To do this, they control the flow of blood to the feet by varying the diameter of the arterial vessels. This is done involuntarily, using the nervous and hormonal systems. In very cold conditions, the flow of blood to the feet is reduced, which minimizes heat loss. In cases when the penguin needs to cool down, the blood flow to its extremities is increased and the penguin's core temperature is reduced, making warm blood go to the feet.

To keep the feet just above freezing point, the blood vessels running to and from the penguin's feet allow for heat exchange. This means that the arteries carrying warm blood to the feet run alongside the veins carrying cold blood up from the feet. Some of the heat from the arteries is transferred to the veins, which helps warm the blood moving toward the heart. At the same time, warm blood moving toward the feet is cooled, keeping the feet at a temperature just above freezing. This minimizes heat loss while also preventing frostbite.

But sometimes the ice can just get a bit too cold to bear. In extremely cold conditions, the penguin will stand on its heels and use its tail to balance in a resting position, allowing it to curl its toes up off the ground for some welcome relief.

⇨ Why Do Gazelles Periodically Leap in the Air When Being Chased by Predators?

Watch an animal documentary set in Africa, and you will often see gazelles springing in the air if they are being chased by a predator. They tend to lift all four feet off the ground simultaneously, holding them in a stiff position while arching their back and pointing their head downward. Such a practice makes the gazelle more visible and uses up valuable time and energy when it could be getting farther away from the danger. This has led scientists to question why they do it—there must be a benefit.

A number of explanations have been proposed for this irregular quadruped behavior known as stotting.

Some claim that it aids in the escape, and that the gazelle is jumping over obstacles. Others say it is used to get up high to detect predators, or that it is an alarm signal to other members of the herd. Still others say that it is a fitness display to potential mates. None of these theories are likely. Stotting usually takes place during an attack, when the predator has been seen and the entire herd is running for its life. There are three more realistic theories.

It confuses the predator. If a number of gazelles start stotting, a pursuing predator might have difficulty picking out an individual to chase. One study on stotting found that when hunting, wild dogs were, in fact, less likely to kill a gazelle when pursuing a herd in which more individuals stotted.

It is a predator detection signal. Stotting might be the gazelle's way of telling the predator that it has been seen and has lost the advantage of surprise, thereby discouraging it from pursuing the gazelle. This would benefit both animals,

saving the gazelle from fleeing and saving the predator from wasting time stalking. Evidence has shown that cheetahs are more likely to abandon a hunt when a gazelle stots from the outset.

It is an honest signal of fitness. Gazelles might stot to indicate to the predator that the gazelle is fit and is not worth chasing. The gazelle is effectively saying that it is so fit and fast that it can escape even if it slows itself down by stotting. This theory is widely accepted, and gazelles that stot for a longer proportion of time in a chase have been found to be less likely to be killed by wild dogs.

⇨ Why Does Spicy Food Make the Eyes and Nose Water?

A common symptom of eating spicy food is watering of the eyes and nose. This is caused by two different chemicals, depending on the type of food eaten.

When it comes to chili peppers, it's capsaicin. Capsaicin is an alkaloid substance contained primarily in the membrane of the pepper that the seeds attach to. Capsaicin exists to deter mammals from eating the fruit. It stimulates nerve receptors in the tongue that sense heat and pain, causing a burning sensation. It is also a key ingredient in pepper spray.

Allyl isothiocyanate is a colorless oil found in mustard, horseradish, wasabi, and radishes. Like capsaicin, it acts as a defensive mechanism against mammals. It is also used as an ingredient in insecticides and fungicides.

Both capsaicin and allyl isothiocyanate cause a burning sensation on your tongue, and they also irritate the mucous membranes in your nose. The membranes become inflamed, which triggers them to produce extra mucus. This is a defense mechanism against the unwanted substance causing the irritation, preventing it from entering your respiratory system. The membranes in your eyes also get irritated by these chemicals, causing your tear ducts to produce more fluid in an attempt to wash the irritant away. The more irritated your nose and eyes become, the more liquid they produce in defense.

Various tissues in your body, such as your intestines, are also irritated by capsaicin and allyl isothiocyanate. The irritation causes the body to try to flush them out, which sometimes results in diarrhea.

The best way to nullify these symptoms is by drinking milk. Both chemicals have an oily quality that renders water ineffective. Milk, however, contains the protein casein, which is a lipophilic molecule that binds to the heat-forming molecules and washes them away. Eating sugar can also produce a chemical reaction that reduces the heat.

⇨ Why Do Old Men Wear Their Pants So High?

It is a universal characteristic of little old men everywhere in the world, regardless of culture: They pull those pants up as high as they'll go. It doesn't look comfortable, and it certainly doesn't look good, so why on earth do they do it?

There are two reasons: fashion and physiology.

Waistlines in men have been moving up and down for centuries. Pantaloons, the early trousers from 18th-century Western Europe, were high-waisted and made with light fabric to elongate a man's figure. During the 19th century, trousers were lower but were often held in place by suspenders. By the 1950s, trousers were generally worn with a belt, but they sat up high above the hips. The men of the time considered it fashionable to have their pants up so high. Those men are now little old men, and have just not changed the way they dress.

Then there are the changes in the old men themselves. Men shrink with age, but they're still wearing the same old pants. This makes their pants too long, meaning they will drag on the ground unless pulled up higher.

As men age, they also lose muscle mass in the glutes. This means their belts don't have a place to rest and won't stay on the waist as easily. To combat this, old men pull their pants up above their hips in an attempt to keep them in place. In addition to this, men tend to become fatter with age. Because their pants won't stay in place under their stomachs, the old men pull them up over the stomach to keep them in place.

Is there a way around this unsightly phenomenon? Yes. Men can exercise to reduce stomach fat and build up the glute muscles, buy pants that fit, or wear suspenders. Or, they can just keep doing what they're doing—there's a lot to be said for consistency. And it has to be better than what's in store for us. By the year 2070, the little old men will be wearing their pants down around their knees, exposing all their underwear.

⇨ Why Does Filipino Start With an F?

Somebody who is Filipino comes from the Philippines. Why does the country begin with "Ph," while the word for someone who lives there begins with an "F"? And why are there two "p"s in the middle of Philippines, but only one in Filipino?

Filipino is derived from Las Islas Filipinas, the name given to the archipelago in 1543 by the Spanish explorer Ruy Lopez de Villalobos. He named it in honor of Felipe II, the King of Spain at the time. When the name of the islands was translated into English, they became the Philippine Islands, spelled with a "Ph" to match the English spelling of Philip. It was also spelt with a double "p" to make it consistent with the English grammatical principles that would give it the correct pronunciation.

But while the country became the Philippines, English didn't have a suitable equivalent for Filipino. "Philippine" and "Philippian" didn't have a good ring to them, so the Spanish word Filipino was adopted into English, retaining the original spelling, as well.

⇨ Is There Any Science to Déjà Vu?

Déjà vu is when a person gets a strong feeling that what they're currently experiencing has happened to them before, even though they know it hasn't. It is a French phrase that translates as "already seen," and was named by the French scientist Émile Boirac in 1876. Around 70 percent of people admit to having experienced déjà vu, yet it is a little understood phenomenon with over 40 theories to explain it, ranging from reincarnation to the existence of multiple universes.

The most cogent theories are memory-based and dream-based.

Some scientists believe that déjà vu involves an anomaly of the memory that can occur when information that was learned but later forgotten is still stored in the brain. When the person experiences similar occurrences, latent memories are triggered. This gives a feeling of familiarity, but it is not familiar enough that you can connect the present to something you've experienced before. This may happen when you see something you have seen before, either in real life or on television or in a photo, but just don't remember it.

The dream-based explanation is of a similar ilk. This theory is that a person may have dreamed about a similar situation or place to that being currently experienced. The person cannot remember the dream, but it is invoked by the real situation, leading to an eerie sense of familiarity.

It is easy to see how some people attribute déjà vu to paranormal or extrasensory forces, but it's almost certainly related to the internal workings of our brains—scientists just can't explain exactly how.

⇨ Why Do Snakes Dart Out Their Tongues?

The flicking tongue of a snake, darting in and out of the mouth, is enough to send chills up the spines of many people. However, contrary to what some people think, it is not a threatening gesture. The

snakes are just "tasting" the air—or rather, they're smelling it.

To compensate for their limited hearing and poor eyesight, snakes have an excellent sense of smell. While they have nostrils to detect scents, they also use their tongues for this purpose.

When a snake's tongue darts out of its mouth, it is getting a better sense of its surroundings by collecting miniscule moisture particles from the air or ground. These particles contain the scents of nearby predators or prey. However, the tongue itself does not have receptors to taste or smell. These receptors are in the vomeronasal, or Jacobson's, organ, which is located inside the roof of the snake's mouth. The prongs of its forked tongue fit into two holes in the Jacobson's organ, where the scent particles are deposited. The chemicals from these particles evoke different electrical signals that are then relayed to the brain, which interprets the sensory information as certain smells.

When following the scent trail of their prey, snakes simply touch the tips of their tongues to the ground to pick up the chemical information. Some snakes also do this to follow the pheromone trails of female snakes.

Because it is forked, the snake's tongue can collect information from two different places at once. This helps them to detect the contours of the land and gain a sense of direction. In essence, their tongues allow them to smell in three dimensions.

⇨ Why Do You Often See a Single Shoe Lying on the Side of the Road?

Known as "the one shoe phenomenon," it is uncanny how often you see a lone boot or shoe lying on the side of the road. And the most puzzling thing is that the shoe is normally in a very noticeable place, like the middle of a busy intersection. Why does this happen? Where is the other shoe?

There are a number of hypotheses about why this happens with footwear more than other types of clothing, and why it happens at all.

Shoes, particularly leather ones, are more sturdily made than other types of clothing, so they will last a long time after being abandoned outside. Shoes are far easier to remove than other clothing, and their absence does not leave the  wearer as embarrassingly exposed as does removing a shirt or a pair of pants. Shoes are also the easiest piece of clothing to throw.

By why are they out there in the first place?

Officials at both the United States Department of Transportation and the National Highway Traffic Safety Administration are aware of the presence of abandoned shoes, but they have not offered an explanation. Here are a few possible theories.

- They fall out of garbage trucks.
- They are one of a pair of shoes cut away from the back bumper of a newlywed car.
- They come loose when people dangle their feet from car windows.
- Both shoes are abandoned but become separated when one rolls away.
- Dogs take one shoe, and, tired of gnawing on it, leave it by the road.

While some shoe abandonment is probably accidental and caused by one of the above reasons, the most likely explanation is that the shoe has been thrown there on purpose.

The most cogent theory is that they're thrown out of school buses or cars during fights or as practical jokes. There is a certain thrill in throwing an object from a moving vehicle, and shoes make useful projectiles, as they can be thrown a distance from the car to avoid detection from authorities. And the more noticeable the placement of the shoe, the more satisfying the act.

Given that many people now discuss the strange concept of the lone abandoned shoe when they see one, the phenomenon has become self-perpetuating, and it's likely that an even higher percentage of shoes will suffer this ignominious fate.

⇨ Why Are the Dates in Movies and Television Shows Written in Roman Numerals?

At the very end of a movie or television show, at the bottom of the credits, you will usually see some Roman numerals appear briefly. These numerals signify the copyright date of the production. Given that they are only on the screen for a couple of seconds and are very hard to translate in that time, why don't they just put the year in numbers?

They're difficult to read for that very reason: The film producers don't want you to read them.

The practice began in an attempt to disguise the age of the show, and it has persisted through to today. Filmmakers believe that the public prefers to watch new material, which is fresh and exciting, and would be less likely to watch a show or movie if they knew it was made years before. In the time that the numerals appear on the screen, it is very hard to translate them into a year, so viewers don't know when the show was made.

There are other, more practical reasons for using Roman numerals. With movies produced on reels of film, the physical film can degrade over time, making it difficult to read numbers, with certain digits such as 5 and 6 appearing the same. Roman numerals prevent this problem. Even without the effect of weathering, Arabic numbers are sometimes difficult to distinguish from each other, a problem that is also averted by the use of Roman numerals.

Then there's the other, less scientific reason: That's just the way it's always been done.

⇨ How Did the Dollar Symbol Originate?

The dollar sign ($) is used to indicate various currencies around the world, most notably the United States dollar. There are a number of theories as to its origin.

One theory is that it came from the Spanish coat of arms, which shows the Pillars of Hercules and a banner threading between them, forming a shape similar to that of the modern dollar sign. While this is a common hypothesis, it is most likely incorrect.

Another explanation is that it started as a monogram of "US" that was used on bags of money issued by the United States Mint. A capital "U" was superimposed over a capital "S" but the bottom of the "U" disappeared into the bottom curve of the "S," forming the dollar symbol with two visible vertical lines. However, no documentary evidence exists to support this theory, and the dollar sign was in use before the United States was formed.

The dollar sign was actually first used in the 1770s, mainly in business correspondences, in reference to the Spanish American peso. Also known as the Spanish dollar, the peso provided the model for the currency adopted by the United States in 1792.

Pesos were commonly abbreviated to "Ps," and handwritten manuscripts from the late 18th-century show this. It is believed that as time went by, the abbreviation came to be written so that the "S" was on top of the "P," producing a close equivalent to the $ symbol. The symbol was being extensively used by the time the first US dollar was printed in 1875.

⇨ ## Why Do Starving Children Have Bloated Stomachs?

It seems paradoxical that starving children often have bloated stomachs, but there is a reason for it.

The condition results from kwashiorkor, a severe form of malnutrition caused by a protein deficiency. An extreme lack of protein in the diet causes an imbalance in the gastrointestinal system, as well as irregularities in the lymphatic system. The main functions of the lymphatic system are waste and toxin removal, fluid recovery, and the absorption of lipids, or fats, out of the digestive tract. Fluid recovery, an important process to help prevent dehydration, is achieved by the reabsorption of water and proteins, which are returned to the blood. A severe state of undernourishment results in low lipid absorption, and an inability to recover fluids. This means that the body is unable to adequately empty its liquid wastes, which accumulate in the stomach, making it distended. The lack of protein also leads to a loss of muscle mass, resulting in weak abdominal muscles that allow the stomach to more easily distend.

While a bloated stomach is the most obvious sign of the condition, other symptoms include tooth and hair loss, loss of appetite, loss of skin pigmentation, and a swelling of the feet and ankles.

Children are more susceptible to kwashiorkor.

⇨ How Did a White Flag Come to Represent a Truce?

The white flag is a sign used to indicate a surrender, truce, cease-fire, or request for negotiation. Waving it indicates that the bearer is unarmed and does not pose a threat. It is an internationally recognized symbol, but how did it originate?

Soldiers have been using white flags as symbols of capitulation for thousands of years. The flag was first used to indicate surrender during the Eastern Han Dynasty, which lasted from 25 AD to 220 AD. The color white was associated with death and mourning in China, so the soldiers may have adopted the white flag to show their sorrow in defeat.

The white flag also arose independently in the Roman Empire. It was used in the surrender of Vitellian forces during the Second Battle of Cremona in the 1st century AD, as recorded at the time by the historian Cornelius Tacitus.

As white cloth was fairly common in ancient times, it is thought that soldiers would improvise with what they had on hand. The practice of using white continued through to medieval Western Europe, where not only was the white flag used, but prisoners captured in battle would attach a piece of white paper to their helmets and troops that had surrendered would carry white batons. The color white indicated that the person was exempt from combat.

By the 1500s, the white flag was being used in India, and during the American Civil War, soldiers waved white flags of truce before recovering their wounded.

The concept of the white flag was later codified in The Hague and Geneva Conventions of the 19th and 20th centuries, and its improper use contravenes the rules of war and constitutes a war crime.

⇨ How Does an Athlete Get a Second Wind?

When competing in a marathon race, it is common for a runner to look completely exhausted, gasping for air, then a few minutes later appear rejuvenated and running better than ever. Commentators will remark, "He's got his second wind." It sometimes seems almost supernatural, leading people to wonder how it happens.

Scientists do not fully understand what causes an athlete's second wind, but there are a number of theories.

1. Lactic acid release. Our bodies use oxygen to break down energy sources. This normal function is called aerobic metabolism, which does not produce lactic acid. But when we exercise heavily, the body's need for oxygen to produce energy is greater than the oxygen it receives. To continue producing energy in this situation, the body switches to anaerobic metabolism. This provides a short boost in energy, but creates lactic acid as a waste by-product. If the oxygen supply is not quickly restored, the lactic acid accumulates, causing muscle inflammation. When an athlete pushes through the pain of this lactic acid buildup, the body acclimatizes and starts to use oxygen more efficiently. The second wind kicks in when the muscles finally get the oxygen they need and the lactic acid decreases. A combination of these two factors creates a sense of euphoria.

2. Metabolic switching. Our bodies store energy in different ways, with glycogen, a carbohydrate, being the most readily usable form. If the body runs out of glycogen during intense exercise, it may switch its metabolism and tap into other energy sources such as fatty acids or proteins. As the body switches to an alternative energy source, the person suddenly feels energized and gets a second wind.

3. Endorphins. Endorphins are hormones that are produced to reduce pain and help us deal with physically difficult activities. "Runner's high" is the feeling of well-being that a runner experiences after a race is over, and this is credited to endorphins. Some scientists believe that the second wind is a similar concept, and is caused by the early release of endorphins.

While any of these physiological explanations could be the reason for the second wind, many believe it is an entirely psychological situation during which the human body simply responds to a renewed sense of willpower, just like the Little Engine: "I think I can, I think I can."

⇨ How Did the Term "Spaghetti Western" Originate for Western Movies?

The low budget sets, the dubbed voices, the iconic music, the blinding sunlight, the laconic antihero—all essential aspects of the Spaghetti Western.

The Spaghetti Western is a type of Western film that originated in the 1960s. These films were typically low budget and imitated the proven successes of their earlier counterparts. To save on production costs, they were filmed in Spain or Italy, and most were produced and directed by Italians. They often had an American in the main role, and the Italian actors had their voices dubbed in English post-production.

The link between spaghetti, the staple Italian foodstuff, and the Italian filmmakers gave the genre its name. The term Spaghetti Western was coined by the Spanish journalist Alfonso Sanchez in the 1960s and was used by American film critics since that time.

The best known and most successful Spaghetti Westerns were *A Fistful of Dollars* (1964), *For a Few Dollars More* (1965), and *The Good, the Bad and the Ugly* (1966). These were all directed by Italian director Sergio Leone, and all starred a young Clint Eastwood. By the end of the trilogy, the Spaghetti Western genre was famous, and Clint Eastwood had become a household name.

⇨ Do Plants Feel Pain?

The question as to whether plants feel pain has been hotly debated for years. One of the reasons for this is the difference between plant cognition and plant perception.

Plant perception is the ability of plants to sense and respond to the environment. There is no doubt that plants do possess this ability, to varying degrees. Plants react to light, moisture, insects, temperature, and many other factors. Many plants use molecular responses and chemical communications to protect themselves. In some cases, they do this by emitting a poison to ward off insects, or a chemical to attract bees. Wounded tomatoes produce a particular odor as an alarm signal to neighboring plants, which allows them to produce different chemicals in defense against the attacking insects. Sunflowers turn toward the sun, the mimosa plant makes its leaves turn down if they are touched, and the Venus flytrap snaps shut to kill insects that land on it.

A 1997 study on plant perception, conducted at the Institute for Applied Physics at the University of Bonn in Germany, shed even more light on the matter. Using a laser-powered microphone, the researchers found that sound waves are produced by gases that plants release when they are cut or injured. These gases, they said, are the equivalent of us crying out in pain.

While these examples of plant sophistication indicate that plants may be able to experience pain, many scientists assert that plant perception is very distinct from plant cognition. They say there cannot be pain or any emotion without a brain to register these feelings. Plants do not possess a nervous system, and without one, plants have neither a mechanism for feeling pain, nor the ability to experience emotions such as suffering. It is purely chemistry that dictates plant behaviors and reactions, similar to how an involuntary chemical reaction causes human skin to increase melanin production when it is exposed to sunlight.

Because there is no evidence for the presence of neurons in plants, the majority of scientists consider the idea of plant cognition to be unfounded and absurd.

So, while plants can definitely communicate, it is unlikely that they can feel pain in the way we do. That said, we may never know for sure, and a 2014 study at the University of

Missouri, Columbia, found something that very few vegetarians will find appetizing: Plants understand and respond to the chewing sounds made when caterpillars eat them. If that's true, perhaps it's best to avoid any eye contact with the lettuce on your plate.

⇨ Why Do Our Palms Sweat When We Are Nervous?

What do standing on the edge of a cliff, talking in front of an audience, and taking your final exams have in common? They all make your palms sweat. Don't worry; it's a perfectly natural reaction.

Humans have two types of sweat glands: apocrine and eccrine. Apocrine glands are mainly located where we have a lot of hair, such as under the armpits. They produce a thick sweat that results in body odor.

Eccrine glands, however, produce a clear and odorless sweat, and function to control body temperature. They make up most of the sweat glands we have, and their highest concentration is on the forehead, the soles of the feet, and the palms of the hands. The sweat that they produce evaporates, reducing your temperature.

The eccrine glands in your palms are stimulated by the sympathetic nervous system. In order to reduce your temperature, they get a signal from the hypothalamus region of the brain. But when you are nervous or excited, regardless of whether you are hot or not, the signal from the brain that tells your eccrine glands to produce sweat comes from the neocortex and limbic centers.

Why would the same reaction be produced, using the same system and glands, for completely different reasons?

It's done for efficiency. When emotional stress causes sweaty palms, it can help control the humidity of the outer layer of the skin. For our ancestors, a mild amount of sweat on the palms that was readily evaporated would have improved hand friction to assist in grasping a spear for a hunt, fighting enemies, or climbing for food or safety. At the same time, the hypothalamus then sends a signal to produce more sweat to help the body to cool down from these intense activities.

For modern-day man, however, the two functions don't necessarily go hand in hand, as a job interview, for example, would rarely develop into a physical contest. Still, we get the sweaty palms anyway.

So, the next time you're standing on the edge of a cliff and get sweaty hands, just panic about falling off, and don't worry about your palms. That sweat is just your body functioning normally.

⇨ Who Invented the Wheel?

"We don't need to reinvent the wheel" is a commonly heard expression. But do the users of this hackneyed phrase ever wonder who actually invented the wheel in the first place?

The wheel is a relatively new invention. Animal domestication predates the wheel, as does the practice of agriculture, which is thought to have begun in around 12,000 BC.

Archaeologists and historians believe that the vehicular wheel was invented by various different cultures in different geographical locations—the ancient Sumerians of Mesopotamia, the Maykops of Northern Caucasus (the border of Europe and Asia), and the Cucuteni-Trypillians of Central Europe—at about the same time, in around 3,500 BC. But we don't know who actually got there first.

It is believed that the wheel came about as a series of slow incremental advances, and its delay was related to the fact that the wheel itself is fairly useless unless it can be combined with an axle to stabilize it. Metal tools were required to build such a device, and these didn't become widespread until about 4,000 BC.

The oldest functioning wheel-axle combination was found in present-day Slovenia and is dated to around 3,300 BC, while another, where the axle does not rotate, was found in Hungary and dates to 3,200 BC. It is believed that the Chinese didn't have wheeled vehicles until 2,000 BC.

⇨ Is Using a Cell Phone at a Gas Station Actually Dangerous?

If you dare to use your cell phone while filling up at a gas station, other motorists will start jumping up and down and the manager will probably come running out to stop you. There are warnings posted at every station about not using cell phones, and even the cell phone owner's manual states not to use it at a gas station. Using a cell phone at a gas station is obviously extremely dangerous, right?

No, not at all.

Rumors have circulated for years suggesting that using a cell phone in the presence of fuel vapors is highly dangerous. The theory is that an electrical spark from the phone will ignite the vapors and cause a fire or explosion. As a result  of these rumors, and out of an abundance of caution, the gas stations have posted the warnings. But the risk is very, very low, to the point of being minute.

It is theoretically possible to cause a fire with a cell phone. Though there is easily enough energy in the phone's battery to produce a spark to ignite a fire, a phone doesn't produce a spark, and even if the battery did, the spark would likely be too small and would be contained within the phone casing anyway. The lithium battery could also potentially explode while it is charging if the internal circuitry is faulty, but this is very unlikely as well, and you wouldn't normally be talking on a charging phone while pumping gas.

Then there's the electrical field that your cell phone produces. The field has been measured at two to five volts per meter, which has never been known to set off a fire. Nearby cell phone towers create a far greater electrical field and would actually be much more likely to start a fire at a gas station.

So, has a cell phone ever set off a fire at a gas station? No. The Australian Transport Safety Bureau assessed 243 gas station fires worldwide over an 11 year period, and none were caused by cell phones.

Even the United States government agrees that the risks are low. The Federal Communications Commission has concluded that the potential threat is remote, while the Cellular Telecommunications Industry Association has said that there is no evidence at all that a cell phone has caused an explosion at a gas station anywhere in the world. A representative from the American Petroleum Institute reiterated this fact, saying, "We have not found a cell phone responsible for any fire since the beginning of mankind."

So, what's causing the gas station fires? Static electricity, mostly. If a person wearing synthetic clothes in dry weather slides across a fabric car seat, they can build up a significant static charge. If the earthing wire of the pump hose is broken, a visible spark can discharge when the metal nozzle is touched to the metal of the car's tank, which is enough to ignite the gas vapors and start a fire.

But in the end, the cell phone myth is just that—endless chatter. Just make sure it doesn't generate too much static.

⇨ Why Are Easter Eggs Given?

If you think of Easter, candy Easter eggs are one of the things that tends to spring to mind. It's that time of the year when chocolate seems to be everywhere, and it's hard not to gorge yourself during the four-day holiday. Given that Easter is a religious celebration, how did chocolate eggs become a part of it?

The egg has long been a symbol of fertility and birth. Hindi scriptures state that the world developed from an egg, and in Egyptian mythology, the phoenix burns its nest and is later reborn from the egg that is left. It is probably from these pagan ideas that Christianity borrowed the concept.

Eggs have been associated with the Christian festival of Easter since the early days of the church. The custom of giving duck or hen eggs at Easter began with the early Christians of Mesopotamia. The egg, as a symbol of new life, represented the empty tomb of Jesus, from which he had resurrected. Originally, the eggs were stained with red coloring in honor of the blood that was shed at his crucifixion. Other Christians regarded the egg as a symbol for the stone that was rolled away from the entrance to Jesus's tomb.

This custom of giving painted eggs then spread to Russia and the Orthodox churches, then into Europe and through the Roman Catholic and Protestant churches.

By the 17th and 18th centuries, egg-shaped toys were given to children at Easter. These were often covered with colored decorations.

It wasn't until the 19th century that chocolate Easter eggs were given in France and Germany. These later developed into the chocolate molded eggs that are given today throughout the world, either left by the Easter Bunny, or hidden for children to find on Easter morning.

⇨ Why Does Time Seem to Fly As We Get Older?

When we were children, summer vacation seemed to last forever. As we get older, it goes in the blink of an eye, leaving us to say comments like, "Where has the year gone?" and "Can you believe it's almost Christmas?" Why does our perception of time speed up with age?

It might make you feel a little better to know that this is a genuine phenomenon—time does seem to speed up. But it is not an exact science, so there are a number of competing theories.

1. Biological clocks. As we age, our metabolism slows, as do our heart rates and breathing. The slowing of this internal pacemaker, relative to the constant pace of real time, makes time seem to pass more quickly.

2. Memorable events. Another theory suggests that our perception of time is related to the number of memorable events we experience. This was first put forward by the American psychologist William James in his 1890 text *Principles of Psychology*. He believed that time speeds up as we age because it is accompanied by fewer and fewer memorable events. This lack of new experiences makes the days, weeks, and years smooth themselves out and pass in a blur. James went on to say that we might measure past intervals of time by the number of key events that can be recalled in that period. When we are young, numerous such events can take place in a short space of time (first kiss, learning to drive, graduation), making it feel much longer than it really was.

3. New stimuli. Similar to the memorable events theory, this hypothesis suggests that time is related to the amount of new information we receive. When faced with new situations, our brains record those memories in great detail. Everything is new when we are young, requiring us to use more brainpower to take it in. This makes time seem to pass more slowly. As we age, we become familiar with our surroundings and don't notice the details of our environments, making time run faster. It has been suggested that the neurotransmitter dopamine is released when we see novel stimuli, and our levels of dopamine drop as we age, making time speed up.

4. Attention. As we age, we tend to pay less attention to time. Kids are always counting down the days until their birthday or a vacation, and the time seems to pass slowly. Meanwhile adults, who are busy working and dealing with life, don't focus on time as much. The next thing you know, a year has passed.

5. Proportional theory. The idea behind this theory is that time is measured on a logarithmic scale and that we perceive a period of time as a proportion of the time we have already lived. For a two-year-old, one year is 50 percent of their lives, whereas to an 80-year-old, one year is just over one percent. This makes time seem to accelerate as we get older. On the logarithmic scale, a person would perceive the passage of time between ages one and two the same as they would perceive the passage of time between ages 10 and 20, or 20 and 40.

So, it turns out that the expression isn't quite right after all—time flies, whether you're having fun or not. And, unfortunately, it flies faster and faster every day.

⇨ Is the Tomato a Fruit or a Vegetable?

Old Satchmo, the great Louis Armstrong, once sang, "You like tomato, and I like tomahto," in reference to how the vegetable should be pronounced. But it's not just the pronunciation that causes arguments; it's also whether the tomato is actually a vegetable at all.

It all depends on how you look at it.

The tomato consists of the ovary of a flowering plant and contains the plant's seeds. Botanically and scientifically speaking, this makes the tomato a fruit.

However, the tomato is not very sweet, as it has a much lower sugar content than most fruits. As a result, it is typically served as part of a main meal or salad, rather than as a dessert. In the culinary world, this makes it a vegetable.

What this means is that the tomato is technically a fruit, but practically a vegetable. This categorization also applies to cucumbers, green beans, bell peppers, squashes, and eggplants.

The tomato's classification actually led to a legal dispute in the United States in 1887. Tariff laws imposed a duty on vegetables, but not fruits. The Supreme Court settled the point in 1893, declaring the tomato to be a vegetable, based on the popular definition that classifies vegetables by use.

Case closed. "Let's call the whole thing off."

⇨ What Caused the 2008 Global Financial Collapse?

Considered by many economists to be the worst financial crisis since the Great Depression of the 1930s, the global financial crisis of 2008 had causes both multiple and complex. Though books have been written about the events, here it is in a nutshell.

From 1997 to 2006 in the United States, housing prices were on the rise. Credit was easy to get and people bought expensive houses that were heavily mortgaged. The lending companies were making a lot of money at this time, and, expecting house prices to keep rising, they made it easier for people to get loans, even though the people couldn't necessarily afford them. These loans were called subprime loans. In

an attempt to sign more loans, the lending companies offered low initial interest rates that would later increase.

While housing prices were still booming, many American and European companies and banks invested in the sub-prime loans, buying them in large packages. Caught up in the frenzy, the housing companies built too many houses, and this surplus caused the prices to drop. By March 2008, the value of many homes—as many as 8.8 million—had dropped to below the remaining value of the mortgage debt owed by the homeowners. After their interest rates had risen, owners were unable to sell their houses or meet the repayments, and the banks foreclosed on millions of properties. The number of houses for sale continued to increase, making prices decrease further. The housing bubble burst and the value of the packaged subprime investments decreased. Large companies, including Citigroup and Merrill Lynch, lost around $512 billion in total.

Financial institutions around the world were damaged, and questions arose regarding bank solvency. The availability of credit declined massively, and a lack of investor confidence made global stock markets plummet.

As credit availability tightened, international trade declined, and governments provided unprecedented bailout packages to large financial institutions. Trillions of dollars were lost, and the global economy was worse than it had been for 80 years.

⇨ Why Is 666 Considered the Devil's Number?

The number 666 has long been considered the number of evil, or the devil's number. This stems from the *Bible*.

In the Book of Revelation in the New Testament (13:15-18), 666 is associated with the Beast of Revelation. The number is only mentioned once, but it is referred to as the number of a man associated with the Beast.

The Beast may refer to one of two mythological creatures described in the Book of Revelation. One comes out of the sea, and the second out of the earth. This second beast, referred to as the false prophet, directs all people to worship the first

beast. They are both in opposition to God, but are both defeated by Christ and thrown into a lake of fire.

As a result of these Bible extracts, 666 is widely recognized as the mark of the Antichrist, or the devil, and has been used on innumerable occasions in popular culture as a reference to the devil.

Hexakosioihexekontahexaphobia is a word of ancient Greek origin that means a fear of 666, and many people avoid things related to that number. In 1989, when Ronald and Nancy Reagan moved from the White House to their home in Bel Air, Los Angeles, they had its address changed from 666 St. Cloud Road to 668 St. Cloud Road.

⇨ Why Do So Many Irish Names Have an "O" in Front of Them?

Have you ever noticed how many Irish names have "O" in front of them? O'Kelly, O'Riley, O'Sullivan…the list goes on. The explanation is simple.

In ancient Ireland, the population was far smaller than it is today, and people tended to live in one town their whole lives. It was usual at the time for a person to be known by just their first name, and because there were so few people in the town, there was rarely any confusion.

As the population of Ireland started to grow during the 11th century, the need for further identification of people arose. The surnames in some countries were created using professions. The Gaelic *clann* system, however, gave people a common identity with others of their tribe and area, so in Ireland, surnames were assigned using personal names.

The simple way of doing this was to add a prefix. "Mac" was added to mean "son of," while "O" was added to mean "descendant, or grandson, of." Someone named O'Connor was the grandson (and later, the descendant) of Connor.

The vast majority of these Gaelic Irish surnames were in place by the 12th century.

⇨ Does a Goldfish's Memory Really Only Last a Few Seconds?

It is a popular belief that a goldfish has a virtually nonexistent memory span, and every lap of the fishbowl is like seeing the world for the first time. It turns out that this is not true—far from it, in fact.

Goldfish are actually very intelligent creatures and have excellent memories. They can be trained to respond to different colors of light and types of music, push levers to receive food, and find their way around mazes. They can even tell the time (sort of). Scientists at the University of St. Andrews in Scotland claim that goldfish are at least as intelligent as rats.

These harmless little fish have been shown to be able to recognize their owners and don't consider them a threat, even if touched by them. They can respond to the appearance and voice of their owners. Yet around strangers, the fish will often hide.

A number of experiments have been conducted to test their intelligence. In one, the fish had to learn to escape a net through a small hole. They succeeded after about five trials, and after a gap of a year, they were able to remember the exact escape route straightaway.

In another experiment, researchers trained goldfish to associate a certain sound with feeding time. The fish were then released into the wild. Five months later, the same sound was broadcast over a loudspeaker and the fish returned to their original feeding place.

In another study, researchers at Plymouth University in England trained goldfish to nudge a lever to get food. When the lever was pressed, food was dispensed. The lever was then set so that food would only be given at the same time every day, for one hour. The fish quickly learned to only press the lever at the correct time, and they ignored it for the rest of the day.

These studies show just how intelligent these animals really are, so the next time someone tells you that you have a memory like a goldfish, take it as a compliment.

⇨ How Does the Date-Rape Drug Work?

Known colloquially as "roofies," Rohypnol is a drug that is known to be used in sexual assaults. While there are other drugs that are also used, Rohypnol got its reputation as the first date-rape drug in the 1990s, when people started surreptitiously dissolving it into drinks in the United States.

Flunitrazepam, the active ingredient in Rohypnol, is a type of benzodiazepine, a class of drugs that depresses the central nervous system. It enters the brain rapidly, binding to receptors on neurons in the brain that use the neurotransmitter called GABA. When GABA binds to the receptors, it inhibits the neurons, reducing their activity. When the benzodiazepine is also bound, it enhances the effect of GABA, increasing the GABA and further reducing brain function.

Rohypnol is effectively a tranquilizer about 10 times stronger than Valium, and it renders the victim incapable of resisting. Users often describe a paralyzing effect, with a loss of muscle control and drowsiness. Often, the person will lie on the floor with their eyes open, able to observe events but unable to move.

The effects begin about 20 minutes after taking the drug, peak within two hours, and may last for up to 12 hours. The drug also impairs memory, so the user cannot usually recall anything that happened.

While Rohypnol is sold in Europe and Latin America as a sleeping pill, it is illegal in the United States. Its use in sexual assaults is now considered fairly rare.

⇨ What Does the "D" in D-Day Stand For?

D-Day is a military term used to refer to the day on which an operation is to take place. The most famous D-Day in history is June 6, 1944, which was the day of the Normandy landings in World War II. It was on that day that the Allies began their effort to liberate Europe from the Nazis. Why was it called D-Day?

There are a number of explanations for the "D" in D-Day. Decision Day, Deliverance Day, and Designated Day are just a few. They are all incorrect.

D-Day and H-Hour stand for the day and hour on which an operation is to be initiated. They are used when the exact day and hour have not yet been designated, or when secrecy is essential. The D is simply a placeholder for the actual date, and stands for "date" or "day."

D-Day is sometimes used in combination with numbers, so that D+4 Day means four days after D-Day, and D-2 Day indicates two days prior.

The earliest use of D-Day by the United States Army was during World War I. A US Army Field Order dated September 7, 1918 stated, "The First Army will attack at H hour on D day with the object of forcing the evacuation of the St. Mihiel Salient."

Because D-Day is so closely associated with the Normandy landings, some later military operations have avoided the term to prevent confusion, using other letters. The Allies' planned invasions of Japan in World War II were to take place on X-Day and Y-Day.

⇨ Why Do Sound Check Guys Only Say "Check One, Two"?

"Check, one, two, two, two, check, check, two, two." This is all you ever hear when a band is testing their gear when setting up to play in a bar. Why does the sound check engineer say this? And why doesn't he ever get to three?

There are two words to explain this behavior: sibilance and plosives. Now to explain them.

Sibilance refers to the hissing sound produced by strongly stressing consonants when using words with an "s" in them.

This occurs in a range of frequencies that come off sounding harsh or scratchy. Similar uses of "ch" can also reveal sibilance, especially when the "ch" is drawn out, as in "chhhcck, one, two."

Plosives refer to a consonant that is said by stopping the airflow using the lips, teeth, or palate, then suddenly releasing the air. This bursting release of the consonant gives a hard popping sound. The "ck" at the end of "check" and the "tw" at the start of "two" produce these popping sounds.

Both sibilance and plosives can create thick feedback in the sound system, so when they are heard during testing, the sound engineer can adjust the equipment to compensate.

Saying "check, two, two," is the perfect way to test the system. There is the sibilant "chhh," a plosive "k," followed by the plosive "tw." Pitching down on the "oo" in two then allows you to cover most of the audio spectrum.

The "one" is not of much help at all, and is only there to get to the "two," and there's no point ever making it to "three." So it looks like "chhheck, one, two, two, two, check, two, two," as annoying as it is, is here to stay.

⇨ Why Do We Have 10 Fingers and 10 Toes?

As soon as a baby is born, the first thing a parent checks is that the baby has 10 fingers and 10 toes. Why is that number so important?

Scientists don't know exactly why, but they do agree that 10 toes and 10 fingers are the perfect amount. Why? Because that's how we've evolved. The fact that we have that specific amount means that it somehow gave us an evolutionary advantage.

Including the opposable thumb, having five fingers on one hand gives us the ability to grasp an object perfectly or to make a fist. Generally, for an evolutionary change to develop, the change has to offer some improvement. Given the size of our hands, a sixth finger would not only be redundant, but it would get in the way and actually hinder us.

Some experts believe that we developed 10 toes to aid in balance, and that 10 was the ideal number for that. But that doesn't explain what makes 10 ideal.

One of the leading theories in the area is known as Limb Law. Developed by the theoretical neurobiologist, Mark Changizi, Limb Law is a mathematical formula that explains the number of smaller limbs an animal needs based on the length of its longer limbs. As a rule, the shorter the limb, the more "limbs" are necessary.

Limb Law states that fingers and toes are considered "limbs" of the hands and feet. And the correct number of these shorter limbs, given the length of our hands and feet, is five. On the hands, five is the perfect ratio for grasping objects and making a fist, and on the feet, five is the perfect ratio for balancing, walking, and in the time of our early ancestors, helping to grasp a branch.

⇨ What Makes the Earth Spin?

The earth spins because it always has, even when it was nothing but dust and gas.

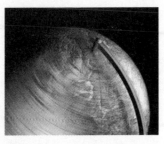

Almost five billion years ago, our solar system began as a vast cloud of dust and gas. The shock wave from a nearby supernova (the explosion of a large star) caused this cloud to collapse inward, flattening it into a giant disk and making it spin. Over time, the dust particles collided into one another and began to stick, forming larger and larger objects in a process known as accretion. The sun formed at the center, and the planets formed around it. As these bodies formed, their momentum was maintained and they began to spin faster and faster as they grew.

As each object formed, it inherited its rotation from the overall movement of the initial cloud of dust. That is why all the bodies in our solar system spin in the same direction.

Scientists believe that a large object collided with earth when it was a young planet, knocking out some material that eventually became the moon. This collision set the earth spinning at a faster rate, but even without any other forces acting on them, the inertia of the sun and the planets has kept them spinning for billions of years. And they will continue to spin unless something disturbs them.

It is thought that the early earth was spinning at such a rapid pace that a day was only about six hours long. However, because of the moon's gravitational pull, the spin of the earth

is slowing down by about one millisecond per year. By the
time the dinosaurs walked the planet, a day was 22 hours
long. Millions of years from now, the length of a day on earth
will stretch out further, getting to 30 and 40 hours, if enough
time passes. Imagine how much you could get done.

⇨ Why Are Some Parts of the Body More Ticklish Than Others?

If someone tickles the bottom of your feet or under your
armpits, you're likely to wriggle, squirm, and go into hysterics.
The same tickle on your back or arm will have no effect at all.
What causes this dramatic difference?

The sensitive areas of our body that are usually the most
ticklish are those that are the least protected and most vulner-
able to attack. The armpit has the axillary vein and artery,
and provides easy access to the heart; the neck contains the
carotid arteries and jugular vein that supply the brain; and
the exposed, unprotected feet contain highly sensitive nerve
receptors that are located close to the skin.

When we are tickled, the increased sensitivity in these key
areas makes the body perceive a threat and helps us to react
faster. An area of the brain called the hypothalamus initiates
the fight-or-flight response and prepares the body for action.

The accompanying laughter also acts as a defensive
mechanism by displaying a sign of submission to an attacker,
while the squirming may be a way of instinctively covering
up the part of the body being tickled, making it less open to
attack.

People who are very ticklish are not weaker, but actually have more developed protective mechanisms.

⇨ Why Can't People Drink Seawater?

The human body depends on salt. It contains electrolytes that carry electrical currents and regulate nerve impulses. It is required for enzyme production and acid to break down our food. Salt is essential to life and good health. Seawater contains a lot of salt, so why can't we drink it?

Because it contains too much salt. The salt content in seawater is much higher than what the body can process. The salinity of human blood is nine grams per 1,000 grams of water. Seawater, however, is a hypertonic fluid, and has a salinity of 35 grams per thousand. Dealing with this level of salt sends the body into disarray.

Our cell membranes are semipermeable, meaning that water can diffuse in and out of the cells, but other substances, such as sodium and chloride (the main components of salt), can't. When the concentration of salt is higher outside our cells than inside, water moves from the inside to correct the imbalance through a process called osmosis. This transfer of water from the cells causes them to shrink.

In an attempt to then eliminate this excess salty fluid from around the cells, the body produces urine. The problem is that the kidneys can only make urine that is less salty than seawater. This means that to remove all the excess salt, more urine is made than the amount of water we actually drank.

The result is disastrous. Dehydration sets in. The body tries to compensate for the fluid loss by increasing the heart rate and constricting blood vessels in order to maintain blood pressure and flow. The depleted body fluids result in muscle cramps and a lack of blood to the brain and other organs. This eventually leads to coma, organ failure, and death. Don't drink seawater.

⇨ How Do Candles That Don't Blow Out Work?

It's been a staple joke at birthday parties for years: It's time to blow out the candles on the cake, and the guest of honor is left exasperated and embarrassed as the candles keep coming back to life. But how is this possible?

In a normal candle, the hot wick melts the wax and absorbs the liquid wax, pulling it upward. The flame then vaporizes the wax, and this vapor burns and keeps the candle alight. When the candle is blown out, a wisp of smoke rises from the wick. That's the last bit of wax vapor escaping. There is a small ember left in the wick, but without the flame, there is not enough heat to ignite the vapor and continue the burning process.

With a trick candle, the idea is to ensure there is enough heat to ignite the escaping vapor and bring the flame back to life. Magnesium is a highly flammable metal that ignites at very low temperatures. Powdered magnesium is put inside the wick so that when the candle is blown out, the ember that remains is hot enough to light the magnesium, which then burns the vapor. The flame reappears and the burning process continues.

The reason the magnesium doesn't all burn off straight away is that there is a barrier of wax around the wick, keeping the magnesium cool and away from the oxygen in the air. Once the candle is blown out, the wick becomes exposed and the magnesium is able to ignite.

So, how do you put them out? They need to be snuffed out, or put out with liquid, to cut off the oxygen supply so that the flame can't reignite.

⇨ Why Do Women Live Longer Than Men?

Across the industrialized world, women live, on average, five to ten years longer than men, and of all people over 100 years old, 85 percent are women. There are both physiological and evolutionary theories to account for this gender disparity.

1. Iron. Women don't develop cardiovascular diseases until much later than men do. This is thought to be related to menstruation, which leads to a lack of iron. Iron creates reactions in our cells that produce damaging free radicals and age the cells. This is also the main reason why vegetarians are usually healthier than meat eaters.

2. Stress. As a rule, men do not deal with stress as well as women do. Stress is known to increase the chances of cardiovascular disease, and it also leads to depression. Far more men than women attempt suicide, and if they do, they are far more likely to succeed than women are.

3. Lifestyle. Men generally drink and smoke a lot more than women, and they eat more foods that lead to high cholesterol.

4. Hormones. While estrogen in women is thought to help eliminate bad cholesterol, the higher levels of testosterone in men can lead to violence and risk-taking. Young men are less likely to wear seat belts, and are more likely to have accidents and engage in violent behavior. This leads to a higher death rate in young men than in women. Men are also more likely to neglect their medical care.

5. Evolution. According to an evolutionary theory called the caregiver theory, women live longer than men because women are more essential to the survival and well-being of the children. Women have always done more of the childcare than men, so women evolved to survive longer to maximize the length of time they can raise children, and then assist in raising grandchildren. This theory is demonstrated in other primates, as well. Where childcare duties are equal between the sexes, as with titi monkeys and the siamang gibbon, males and females have the same life expectancy. However, with the South American owl monkey, the male does most of the childcare and nurturing, and generally lives longer than the female.

Will the balance ever be redressed in humans? For the average man's life expectancy to match a woman's, he will have to drink and smoke less, eat less red meat, relax, not take as many risks, and then evolve by looking after the children for a couple hundred thousand years.

⇨ Why Do Some Blind People Wear Dark Glasses?

People tend to associate dark glasses with blind people because a number of blind celebrities have worn them, including Ray Charles and Stevie Wonder. But it's not just a look that they're going for; there are actually a number of reasons for wearing them.

- Many legally blind people are still able to see light, and those that can are often very light-sensitive. Bright light can cause pain and trigger migraines. Because their vision is impaired, they will seldom have a warning that bright light is coming, so dark glasses protect their eyes. The glasses also help reduce the damage that ultraviolet rays from the sun can cause.

- Dark glasses operate to protect a blind person's eyes from obstacles such as hanging tree branches or cupboard doors.

- Some blind people wear dark glasses for aesthetic reasons, because they are self-conscious about the physical appearance of their eyes. Sometimes their eyes may be disfigured or out of focus, and wearing dark glasses prevents other people from staring.

- Wearing dark glasses alerts other people to the fact that a person is blind. This helps to prevent accidents and awkward social situations.

⇨ Why Do Quarterbacks Say "Hut!"?

The word "hut" is an interjection shouted by football quarterbacks to initiate a play. It doesn't mean anything in English, so how did it come about?

Monosyllabic words like hip, hup, and hep have been used for centuries to issue commands to animals. Herders used them for steering sheep, and coachmen called them out to direct their horses. They are short, sharp words that can be heard from a distance.

Drill sergeants in the early 20th century then started using similar words in rhythmic cadences for marching their troops. From the early 1920s, "hip, 2, 3, 4" was commonly used in this regard. By World War II, the sergeants began yelling "Atten-hut!" as a call to attention. The sharp sound of "hut" at the end of the word was used to make a platoon focus and listen.

In football, "hike" was the first of these types of words to be used. Prior to this, the quarterback would usually scratch the center's leg as a signal for the center to give him the ball. But during the 1890-91 season, John Heisman (who later became a football coach and writer) was playing center for the University of Pennsylvania when an intentional leg scratch from an opposing player tricked him into hiking too early. To combat this scurrilous tactic, Heisman introduced the word "hike" to start the snap. The word already meant "to lift up," and was a short, sharp sound that worked well.

With the success of "hike," the similar-sounding "hut" was introduced by the 1950s for the quarterback's cadence in calling the snap count: "Hut 1, hut 2, hut 3." Hut is short and sharp and can be heard clearly over a distance, making it perfect for football. Coming so soon after the war, it is almost certainly derived from the military drill sergeants.

⇨ Why Are Men in Charge of the Barbecue When Women Do Most of the Cooking?

In most households throughout the Western world, the woman is in charge of the kitchen and all the cooking—except when it comes to the barbecue, that is. That's the man's domain. "Women cook, men grill." That's the rule and everybody accepts it. But what is it that makes grilling men's work?

In our early history, women foraged for certain foods, such as fruits, while men went out and hunted dangerous prey that was more difficult to come by. While the women did most of

the cooking, the men tended to cook meat on ceremonial occasions following a big hunt. This has filtered through to modern times, where barbecuing is often seen as a sense of occasion.

Added to this is the thrill of grilling. It involves fire and sharp tools, adding an element of danger to which the testosterone-filled man is drawn. The kitchen is boring, but the barbecue is exciting.

There's also the prehistoric bonding element of gathering around a fire. Grilling provides a good opportunity to hang out with other men and drink beer. The barbecue is seen as the guys' turf—it's their territory, and it acts as a sanctuary where they're able to talk freely among themselves.

Fire, meat, beers, men—these factors all create a strong connection between grilling and masculinity. The barbecue is dangerous, it is the man's domain, and only he shall cook on it.

But the main reason why men only cook on the barbecue and not in the kitchen? The barbecue requires very little in the way of cleaning up.

⇨ Why Are the Upper Class Called Blue Bloods?

A blue blood is a member of a socially prominent and wealthy family, and the term is generally reserved for the upper class of society. The term has existed for centuries, but given that nobody's blood is actually blue, how did it originate?

Blue blood is the translation of the Spanish *sangre azul*, and relates to aristocrats who lived in Castile, Spain, centuries ago.

From their invasion in the 8th century, the Moors, who were from North Africa and had dark skin, ruled over much of Spain. Many interracial marriages took place, but the oldest and proudest families from Castile were quick to boast that they had never intermarried with the Moors or any other race.

As a result, the Castilians were pure and remained extremely fair skinned, making their veins appear a profoundly blue color against their white skin. They took this to be a mark of good breeding and called themselves the *sangre azul*—the blue bloods.

The term was later used in England to describe the nobility, before it became globally recognized.

⇨ Why Is the Moon Sometimes Visible During the Day?

As everyone knows, during the day the sun is the brightest object in the sky, while at night it is the moon. Given that the light from the sun stops us from seeing any stars during the day, why is it that we can often see the moon when the sun is out?

There are two reasons: the moon's luminosity, and the lunar cycle.

The moon is very luminous to us because it is the closest stellar object to the earth. This proximity to the earth, coupled with the sunlight that reflects off the moon's surface, makes it very visible.

But for the moon to be visible in the sky, it needs to be above the horizon. Because of the earth's and the moon's rotation, the moon is above the horizon about 12 hours per day. Some of those 12 hours, usually about six per day, coincide with daylight, making the moon visible during the daytime.

Whether we can then see the moon during the day depends on what phase of the lunar cycle the moon is in. When the moon is approaching the new moon phase, it is too close to the sun for us to see it, as the light from the sun over-powers its reflection. When it is nearing the full moon phase, it is opposite the sun and only becomes visible at night.

The best time to see a daytime moon is during the first and last quarters of its cycle. During these times, the moon is 90 degrees away from the sun, and isn't too close or too far from the sun to be seen by us.

⇨ If Only Female Mosquitoes Bite, What Do the Males Eat?

You walk outside on a hot summer's night and are immediately attacked by a swarm of mosquitoes. Are they really all females? And if they are, what are the males eating?

Yes, they're all females. Only female mosquitoes bite. But blood is not their main food source.

Mosquitoes rely on sugar as their main source of energy, and both males and females feed on plant nectar, mainly from flowers. They use this nectar as fuel to fly and survive, and they replenish it on a daily basis. Mosquitoes actually help pollinate many plant species.

Female mosquitoes don't require blood for survival, but they need it to obtain protein and iron to develop fertile eggs. Nectar lacks these ingredients, so mosquitoes look toward us to get it.

Once the female has obtained some blood, fertilization by the male will occur. Then, she'll rest for a couple of days before laying her eggs.

Those eggs will hatch, the next generation of female mosquitoes will then suck more blood, and the whole process perpetuates, with us as the hapless accessories.

⇨ Why Does Pepper Make People Sneeze?

There are many herbs and spices in the average kitchen, but one spice in particular is notorious for making us sneeze—pepper. Why pepper?

The human nose is designed to repel anything except air. It employs a number of ways to do this. It has nasal hairs in the nostrils that trap particles, it produces mucus, which runs out of the nose to remove foreign objects, and it sneezes.

Known as sternutation, sneezing is a reflex action that expels air from the nose at speeds of up to 100 miles per hour. When the nerve endings in the mucous membrane are irritated, a message is sent to the brain that sends a signal to the relevant muscles to effect a sneeze. This is the body's way of expelling an irritation before it can enter the lungs and cause an infection.

There are two reasons why pepper induces a sneeze.

Pepper is often finely ground, and like any other dust or tiny particle, it can stimulate the nerve endings in the nose and trigger a sneeze.

But chemical composition is the main reason pepper makes us sneeze more than other spices do. Pepper contains a chemical called piperine. Piperine, which gives pepper its spicy flavor, is an alkaloid chemical that is a particular irritant to our nose and quickly stimulates the nasal nerve endings, causing us to sneeze.

And there is no discrimination when it comes to pepper—black or white, they'll both make you sneeze.

⇨ How Does Water Divining Work?

Water divining, also known as dowsing, is a method by which some people claim to be able to locate underground water. It works, allegedly, by walking over an area while holding out an apparatus such as a forked stick or bent rod. The apparatus is said to respond by pointing downward at the point where water is located. Is there any scientific explanation for this phenomenon, or is it a pseudoscience?

It is difficult to objectively determine whether water divining actually works. One theory is that the muscles in the body react to the electromagnetic effect produced by the underground water, and the diviner's stick amplifies this effect. However, a series of experiments conducted in the 1970s by physicists John Taylor and Eduardo Balanovski did not detect the emission of any electromagnetic fields by water diviners.

Many studies have been conducted over the years to determine the success rates of water diviners. In a 1990 study undertaken in Kassel, Germany, a $10,000 prize was offered to any successful diviner. All the participants agreed that the test was a fair one, and all expected a 100 percent success rate. The results, however, were no better than chance, and nobody was awarded the prize.

In another study conducted by Hans-Dieter Betz in Munich, Germany, in 1987, 500 diviners were tested and the best 43 were selected for further tests. Over two years, 843 tests were carried out, and only six diviners were said to be better than chance. This led the researchers to suggest there is some skill to water divining, but when the results were later assessed by Jim T. Enright, a professor of physiology at the University of California, he concluded that the results of the six best diviners were merely consistent with statistical fluctuations.

In fact, virtually all the studies conducted over the years have shown that water diviners are no more reliable than chance.

Skeptics of the process claim that any success by water diviners can be attributed to the fact that the underground water table is distributed quite uniformly in many areas, making a diviner likely to be successful. Others say that diviners know from their experience and local knowledge where water is likely to be located, and either intentionally or subconsciously cause a reaction in their arms which passes through to their divining apparatus. A subconscious reaction in these circumstances is known as the ideomotor effect, where people's minds can influence their bodies without the person purposefully deciding to take action. By this theory, the diviner's stick is simply a conduit for the diviner's subconscious perceptions and knowledge.

⇨ Can You Swallow Your Tongue?

A number of reports have emerged over the years to the effect that someone was exceptionally drunk and died by swallowing their tongue. Is this possible?

No. There is a structure inside the mouth called the lingual frenulum, which is a mucous membrane extending from the floor of the mouth to the midline of the underside of the tongue. The lingual frenulum attaches the tongue to the floor of the mouth and keeps the tongue in position. This anchoring makes it impossible to get the tongue far enough back in the throat to swallow it.

However, depending on the size of the tongue and exactly where the lingual frenulum is attached, it may be possible for a person having a seizure to have their airway blocked by their tongue. But, even then, they can't swallow it.

So, contrary to popular belief, it is not possible to swallow your tongue. Unless, of course, it is cut out first, but this isn't the time or the place to be thinking about Dr. Hannibal Lecter.

⇨ Does Lightning Ever Strike the Same Place Twice?

Everyone has heard the old saying "lightning never strikes the same place twice." Myth, or no myth?

Myth. Lightning can strike any location, any number of times.

When a cloud becomes electrically charged and the field of energy between the two ends of the cloud is strong enough, a discharge called a stepped leader starts from the cloud to the ground, zigzagging down in progressive steps.

Once the stepped leader is close to the ground, a "streamer" of the opposite charge shoots up from the ground or from something on the ground. This closes the circuit and triggers a rush of electricity in the form of a lightning bolt.

And lightning has no memory. If an object has been struck once, it is no less likely to be struck a second time. Tall objects such as skyscrapers, radio towers, or mountains are more likely to be struck repeatedly because their streamers narrow the gap between the ground and the cloud above, making them better targets.

The Eiffel Tower has been struck by lightning many times, and the shuttle launch pad at Cape Canaveral in Florida gets repeatedly hit, sometimes more than once in the same storm. The Empire State Building in New York City gets struck by lightning about 25 times each year.

That said, it's not just tall buildings that lightning strikes. It can strike low objects as well, even flat ground, or people. And it can do so more than once.

If you don't believe that, you should talk to Roy Sullivan (if he were still alive, that is). Roy was a United States park ranger in Shenandoah National Park, Virginia. Between 1942 and 1977, he was struck by lightning on seven different occasions, surviving all of them, and earning him a place in the *Guinness Book of World Records*.

⇨ What Causes Jealousy in a Relationship?

Jealousy can be one of the most detrimental issues in any relationship. And when it is well-founded and a spouse is caught cheating, a relationship will often end. But what causes such intense feelings of jealousy and fear of a partner cheating?

Sexual jealousy exists in animals that reproduce through internal fertilization. It is based on the instinct to guard the gene pool and the expectation that partners will care for offspring. Evolutionary psychologists believe that there is a gender difference in the reasons behind jealousy, and that difference is based on biology.

Jealousy in a man is based on his fear of investing in children that are not his. Men do not want to provide resources for offspring that they are not biologically related to; they do not want to be cuckolded. This threat of investing in unrelated offspring is the reason that men feel jealousy most strongly over their partner's sexual infidelity.

Women, on the other hand, are more concerned with emotional infidelity. This is because women are more focused on having a partner to help raise their children. A sexual indiscretion by a man does not necessarily threaten his parental investment, while a deep emotional attachment to another woman makes it more likely that he will focus his resources on her and not on his current children.

Alternative explanations from a social-cognitive perspective exist. Women invest a lot of emotion into a relationship, so if a man connects emotionally with another woman, the original partner will experience a severe threat to her self-perception. Men, however, place a lot of importance on their sexual dominance and masculinity, so if a woman cheats on a man, his ego suffers badly.

⇨ What Makes Drinking Glasses Sweat?

On a hot and humid day, you sit outside and beads of sweat form on your forehead. You pour yourself a cold drink, and very soon, there is moisture on the outside of the glass. You knew it was hot, but is your glass really sweating, as well?

It's not actually sweating. This moisture is caused by a common process called condensation. The air outside contains water vapor, and warm, humid air contains more vapor than cold, dry air.

When the water vapor that surrounds a glass is warmer than the liquid inside it, the vapor forms on the outside of the glass. Warm air has high energy, and the water vapor molecules move quickly. However, when they come into contact with the cold glass, the molecules lose energy, slowing down and getting closer together. If they slow down enough, they turn into liquid droplets on the side of the glass. This is condensation, and it makes the glass appear as if it's sweating.

The same effect happens when sunglasses (or camera lenses) fog up when we move from an air-conditioned room to the hot weather outside. The hot air containing the water vapor condenses on the cool sunglasses and forms very small liquid drops that cover the glasses in a fog. The reason they don't fully sweat is that the temperature difference is not as high as it is between the hot air and a glass containing cold liquid.

⇨ Can You Catch a Disease from a Toilet Seat?

Do you ever find yourself in a public restroom, completely unwilling to touch anything? You push the stall door open with your knee and flush the toilet with your shoe. The germs of chlamydia, gonorrhea, and syphilis are lurking everywhere in there, just waiting to strike. Whatever you do, don't touch a thing, because everyone knows you can catch a sexually transmitted disease from a toilet seat.

You actually can't. Well, you probably can't.

While the bacteria and viruses that cause an STD do commonly exist in public toilets, they can't survive for long after leaving the human body. They are spread through sexual contact or direct skin-to-skin contact and are quite fragile, drying out and dying after a few minutes on a toilet seat.

There is a theoretical risk, but it is remote. For an infection to occur, the germs would have to be transferred from the toilet seat direct to your genital or urethral tract, or at the very least to an open cut on your skin. This would have to happen within a few minutes of the germs arriving on the seat. So, while it is possible, it is very unlikely. As Abigail Salyers, the 2001 president of the American Society of Microbiology, said, "To my knowledge, no one has ever acquired an STD on the toilet seat—unless they were having sex on the toilet seat."

So, what can you catch from those dreaded public restrooms? Quite a few other things. Various gastrointestinal viruses such as the norovirus can linger for as long as two weeks on toilet seats contaminated with an infected person's feces. Streptococcus, a species of bacteria that can cause bronchial pneumonia, influenza, and the common cold, is also commonly found in restrooms and can be contracted directly from them.

The best way to avoid these infections is to wash your hands thoroughly with soap after visiting a public restroom; or, better still, hold on until you get home.

⇨ What Makes a Boy's Voice "Crack" at Puberty?

As an adolescent male, there is nothing more embarrassing than this scenario: Relieved that your voice is finally getting deeper, you go to say something in front of a group of people and the noise that comes out of your mouth sounds like Mickey Mouse on helium. What's going on?

As a boy goes through puberty, the larynx (or voice box) grows thicker and larger. This happens with girls, too, but the change is more significant in boys. The vocal cords are two muscles that stretch across the larynx and allow us to speak. When a person speaks, air from the lungs makes the vocal cords vibrate. As they vibrate, they produce pulses of air that result in the sound of the voice.

The pitch of the voice is controlled by how tightly the vocal cords contract as the air hits them. The higher the tension, the higher the pitch. It's a lot like a guitar string. A tight string produces a high pitch.

Before puberty, a boy's larynx is small and his vocal cords are thin, resulting in a high-pitched voice. With the increase in testosterone that puberty gives him, the cartilage of the larynx lengthens, and the vocal cords lengthen and thicken. This makes the voice deeper. The facial bones also grow during this time, creating larger cavities that give the voice room to resonate.

For a period of a few months, while these changes are taking place, a boy's voice may crack or break. This happens because the body has not adapted to the sudden changes, and the boy has difficulty controlling his voice. This usually only lasts a few months, by which time the larynx and vocal cords have finished growing, and the boy has adjusted and can speak normally again, just deeper than before.

⇨ Why Do Gas Tank Gauges Take Longer to Go from Full to Half-Full Than Half-Full to Empty?

It's a common complaint of motorists—you drive for hours and hours before the gas tank gauge gets to half-full, then before you know it, it's about to hit empty. Is this a trick of the mind, or does it actually happen that way?

It does happen that way, and here are the reasons why.

1. The shape of the tank. In many cars, gas gauges are controlled by a floating ball with a weight that is attached to a metal arm. When the ball is floating at the top, the gauge shows "full," and when it's at the bottom, the gauge shows "empty." However, this mechanism measures the depth of the fuel in the tank, not the amount. Many gas tanks are not a uniform shape, and if the tank is wide at the top and narrow at the bottom, in a V-shape, the gauge will drop slowly at first and more quickly as the gas gets lower.

2. Filling excesses. It is possible to fill the tank beyond the full level on the gauge. When the pump clicks off, you can always get another gallon or two in there, which many

people do. This gives you a couple of bonus gallons that the gauge doesn't know are there, meaning that the first bit of gas used doesn't make the gauge move. Then, at the other end, there are a couple of gallons left at the bottom of the tank when the

gauge hits empty. Tanks are designed this way in an attempt to stop people from overfilling (which can cause problems), or running out of gas.

These two factors make the gauge reduction speed vary more considerably from full to half-full than from half-full to empty. To put it into numbers, if a tank holds 30 gallons, the gauge will show full at 28 gallons and empty at 2 gallons, with half-full being 14 gallons. This means that 16 gallons have to be used before the gauge gets to half-full, then after only another 12 gallons it will read empty. In addition, many people don't run their tank down to empty, which means draining the second half will seem even quicker.

3. A manufacturer's trick. Some believe that car manufacturers make the gauges this way on purpose so that people, especially when test driving a car, don't see the needle suddenly drop. This may create a perception of low gas mileage and deter a potential buyer.

4. It's psychological. We've all heard the expression "a watched pot never boils." Well, the opposite is true of a gas gauge. A driver who is conscious that the car's gas is getting low will have a tendency to constantly watch the gas gauge. This will make it feel like it's going down much faster than when the tank was full and there was nothing to worry about.

⇨ How Does Aspirin Find the Pain?

Aspirin is probably the most well-known painkiller available. But how does it pinpoint the exact location of the pain?

Aspirin belongs to a class of drugs called COX-2 inhibitors. When cells are damaged, they produce an enzyme called cyclooxygenase-2, or COX-2. This enzyme produces chemicals called prostaglandins, which send pain signals to the brain. Prostaglandins are unsaturated fatty acids that the cells of the body secrete to cause pain and inflammation to highlight the area of injury. They also cause the damaged area to release fluid to create a protective cushion. This results in swelling.

Aspirin is a derivative of salicylic acid, which comes from willow and birch bark. It works by blocking the COX-2 enzyme. When we take aspirin, it dissolves in our stomachs then travels throughout the bloodstream. When it gets to the site of the cell damage, it binds to the COX-2 enzymes and stops them from working and producing prostaglandins. When no prostaglandins are manufactured, the damaged area does not become inflamed, and there are no more pain signals sent to the brain.

⇨ Why Are Most Babies Born with Blue Eyes?

While only one in five white adults in the United States has blue eyes, most are born with blue eyes. There is a scientific reason for this.

Our eye color has to do with the amount of melanin we have. Melanin is a brown pigment molecule that colors our skin, hair, and eyes. The iris of our eyes is the area that contains the pigment, which is thought to help protect the eyes from the sun. The more melanin you have in your eyes, the darker they are, and the more they reflect sunlight.

Despite the fact that babies inherit eye color from their parents, when they are born they don't usually have the full amount of melanin that they will have as adults. This lack of melanin means their eyes are often blue when they're born. From birth to about the age of two, the amount of melanin gradually increases, leading to a deepening of color. Many babies will have a stable eye color by about six months of age, but some aren't fixed until the age of two.

However, not all babies are born with blue eyes. Babies of Asian, African, or Hispanic descent are often born with brown eyes. This is because they are born with more melanin in their eyes, although their eyes, too, may deepen in color as they age.

Cats also experience this phenomenon, with many kittens being born with blue eyes that later darken.

⇨ Why Do Old Ladies Dye Their Hair Blue?

Known as the blue rinse brigade, elderly women with a blue or purple shade to their hair are a common sight around the Bingo halls. This behavior leads many younger people to ponder, "What would possess an old woman to do this?"

There are two primary explanations for this bizarre practice. One is unintentional, and one is not.

When the hair of older women turns gray, it often takes on a yellowy tinge. To counteract this yellow hue, the women sometimes apply a blue hair rinse. While the process is intended to leave the hair a silvery color, with just a hint of blue, it is often inexpertly and excessively applied, resulting in a very unnatural looking blue.

But there is another, more surprising, reason for the blue hair—fashion. Jean Harlow, the American film actress and sex symbol, had a blue tinge to her hair in the 1930 film *Hell's Angels*. The blue rinse then gained real popularity when it was used by the Queen Mother in Britain just after World War II. An entire generation of older women was drawn to the blue rinse; so drawn, in fact, that they kept it up for 60 years, probably because they were old, and they could.

These days, there are not as many "blue hairs" around. The blue rinse has declined in popularity because better home dyes are available, people are more relaxed about aging and so leave their hair to gray naturally, and the Queen Mother died (as did most of the original blue hair nonagenarians who took to the fashion).

⇨ How Are Bombs Defused?

We've all seen it so many times in the movies: A police officer is sweating as he stands over a bomb, its timer device counting down, while he panics over which wire to cut. Get it right and everyone is saved, get it wrong and...bang!

In the simplest of bombs, like those used in the movies or by many terrorists, a small package of explosives is bundled together with a single blasting cap and an electric detonator. There will also often be a timer and a battery attached to two wires. The way to disarm this sort of bomb is

to cut either of the wires, stop the timer, and pull the cap out of the explosive. A slightly more sophisticated bomb will have its wires contained inside, and one of these must be cut without tripping a tilt switch, which is a hidden wire that, if cut, interrupts the flow of current and activates the detonator.

But this stereotypical situation from the movies rarely materializes. Contrary to popular conception, modern-day bomb disposal experts undertake their task as remotely as they can. Where possible, they will use a remotely controlled vehicle known as a wheelbarrow, which is fitted with cameras, a microphone, and various sensors to detect chemical, nuclear, or biological agents. These remote devices also have the ability to handle and move a bomb. Once the type of bomb is determined, it will be disarmed by replacing previously removed safety features, or jamming or removing parts of the bomb's firing mechanism. Sometimes a bore is cut into the side of a bomb and its explosives are extracted using steam and acid.

If the bomb is not able to be disarmed remotely, a bomb technician will wear a protective suit, similar to a bulletproof vest, and encase the bomb in a containment vessel. The technician will then move away and the bomb will be moved mechanically or detonated within the vessel, vastly reducing the impact of the explosion.

⇨ Why Do Roman and Greek Statues Have No Pupils in the Eyes?

If you're ever in Rome or Greece, it's hard not to be mesmerized by the impressive statues carved so many centuries ago that are still standing today. But while they are impressive, they are equally eerie, with their pupil-less eyes that seem to stare at your every move. People are often left wondering, "Why don't their eyes have pupils?"

Well, they used to. When these statues were made, they were not naked and white like they are today. The entire statue would have been painted, often in gaudy colors, and the eyes were no exception. The eyes were once detailed and lifelike, with colors, and yes, pupils.

Over the centuries, the paint has worn off, leaving the statues with a blank look in their eyes.

By using high-intensity ultraviolet lamps as well as high-resolution cameras, the chemical remains of the minerals and pigments that were used on the statues can be seen. The minerals malachite, azurite, and cinnabar were used for green, blue, and red, respectively, while arsenic compounds were used for orange and charred bone for black.

In other sculptures that were made with bronze, the eye sockets were often left blank and filled with glass, stones, coral, or sometimes jewels to make them seem more realistic. These eyepieces have long since fallen out.

➪ Why Do Most Car Accidents Happen Close to Home?

Various studies have found that around half of all car accidents occur five miles or less from home, and over three quarters of accidents happen 15 miles or less from home. Obviously, a higher percentage of driving is done close to home, but is there any other reason for these disproportionately high figures?

Most experts agree that the main reason we have so many accidents near home is that we're driving in our comfort zone. We feel relaxed because of the repetitiveness of the drive and the familiarity of our local area, and, quite simply, we don't concentrate as much. We know the roads, the turns, the intersections, and the landmarks all so well that sometimes when we arrive home, we can't even remember the drive. It's as if we're on autopilot and we don't focus on the complicated task of driving.

The problem with this is that accidents often happen because of unpredictable events, like the bad driving of another, an animal crossing the road, or a mechanical failure. Vigilance is still needed to deal with these issues, and because we lack it when we're near home, more accidents happen.

We are also more likely to be distracted when we're close to home. We sometimes don't put on the seat belt if we're just going to a nearby store, and we're more likely to talk on a cell phone or scan the radio for music.

On a long drive out of town, however, people tend to be more concerned about safety issues, and this makes them concentrate on their driving. Highway driving is usually on straight roads as well, with fewer obstacles and turns, so the number of accidents per hour of driving is reduced. But as we approach home after a long trip, we often relax as we enter our familiar territory, and that's when problems are more likely to arise.

There is one consolation with all of this. While the vast majority of accidents do happen close to home, they tend to be relatively minor, only resulting in small bumps and scrapes.

⇨ Why Are There So Few Women Pilots?

When was the last time you were on a plane and heard a woman say, "This is your captain speaking?" Never? That's because there are so few women pilots.

The gender disparity in commercial airline pilots is one of the largest of all occupations. According to The International Society of Women Airline Pilots, an overwhelming 97 percent of all commercial pilots are men.

Is this because women just don't like flying, or are there other reasons to explain such a skewed difference?

1. Sexism. Helen Richey was the first commercial female pilot in 1934, but she quit after only 10 months because of how badly she was treated by her male colleagues. Richey was barred from becoming a member of the Pilot's Union and was only permitted to fly in fair weather.

This sexism continued through to the 1970s, when Britain's first commercial female airline captain, Yvonne Pope Sintes, was subjected to sexist treatment from other captains.

Thankfully, sexism in the industry has reduced, so what are the other reasons?

2. Physicality. In years gone by, would-be pilots were subjected to various strength and height requirements, which most women simply could not pass. This prevented women from even training to become pilots in the first place. Again, this is no longer an issue, with prospective pilots being just required to competently fly a flight simulator.

3. The Schedule. Most pilots have a busy schedule and are away from home a lot. This was thought to have deterred many women from flying because they were more focused on family life and staying closer to home.

4. The Dream. A key factor deterring female pilots is that not many little girls dream of being a pilot. It doesn't fit into the typical mold of a female occupation, and is seen as more of a "man's job." There are also very few female role models to look up to and inspire a girl to become a pilot. In a study conducted by British Airways, being a pilot was the second most popular career choice among young boys, while with girls, it wasn't even mentioned.

5. Military Training. The biggest factor against women pilots is thought to be the fact that many pilots come from a military background. This wasn't an option for women in the United States until 1993, when they were first allowed to fly combat aircraft. Before that time, any woman who wanted to become a commercial pilot would have had to pay around $100,000 for the necessary training and experience. This posed a prohibitive barrier for most women.

Now that industry conditions have changed, women can be military pilots, and with the physical restrictions removed, perhaps more women will be flying us around the world before long. All they need is the dream.

⇨ How Did Hunky-Dory Come to Mean "Everything Is OK"?

If someone tells you that everything is hunky-dory, you know that all is fine and okay. But where did this unusual expression originate?

Hunky-dory began with a group of American sailors in the 19th century.

There was a major street in Yokohama, Japan, called Honcho-dori. It was well-known for housing ladies of ill-repute, and when in port after a long voyage, the sailors would frequent the street to partake in the recreational activities being offered.

Hunky, a word that already meant "sexy," was a play on the similar-looking word Honcho, and when "dori" was added, the phrase was spawned.

⇨ When Drinking Alcohol, Why Do People Go to the Toilet More Often After "Breaking the Seal"?

Anyone who's ever had more than a few beers will be familiar with this scenario: You sit in a bar and have a beer, then another couple of bottles, and you're fine. You're about to get your fourth when you are suddenly bursting for the toilet. You go, but soon after you come  back, you have to go again. This happens all night, with you racing off to the toilet to pee every 10 minutes. The longer you can hold off on that first one, the better, because once you break the seal, the floodgates are open.

"Breaking the seal," as it is known, is a physiological phenomenon and has a simple explanation. Alcohol inhibits vasopressin, which is an antidiuretic hormone (ADH). ADH is made in the hypothalamus region of the brain, and is then stored and released from the pituitary gland. The role of ADH is to conserve the body's water by reducing its loss in urine. It binds to receptors in the kidneys and promotes water reabsorption. This means that the volume of urine that is sent to the bladder is less, but more concentrated. Alcohol, however, blocks the nerve channels that produce ADH. This reduces the kidneys' ability to reabsorb water, meaning that excess urine is sent to the bladder. This urine is much less concentrated, but much higher in volume. A full bladder means that you have to go to the toilet more often.

The question then remains, why can you hold off easily for a few beers, but once you go once, it's all over?

It's because it takes some time for the alcohol to suppress ADH and for the lack of water reabsorption to take effect. While drinking the first couple of beers, you still have ADH in your system, so not as much urine is produced. But as you continue to drink, your ADH levels drop. By the time your urine production increases, you will have had a few beers, and it's only then that you have to go for the first time. But by then you have to keep going, because your ADH is severely suppressed and large quantities of urine are being produced.

Any drink that contains carbonation such as beer, champagne, or anything mixed with soda will make the urge to go to the toilet even stronger. This is because the gas from those drinks will increase the pressure in your bladder, which will then feel even more full.

⇨ Why Do Wounds Itch as They're Healing?

As any wound on the skin starts to heal, it itches. Why?

There are two reasons.

1. The skin contains nerve fibers that detect when the dermis (one of the upper layers of the skin) is being irritated. Those fibers then send a signal to the brain telling it that there is an itch. This is known as a mechanical stress, which is done to warn the brain about a potential danger.

When a wound heals, the cells around the wound increase at its base, joining together and contracting to pull the wound shut. This produces a mechanical stress similar to an irritation. The nerve fibers alert the brain, which results in an itch.

2. The body releases a chemical called histamine in response to a wound in an attempt to prevent bacteria from entering the wound. The histamine is released at the site of the wound, and because it is not normally found there, its presence stimulates the nerve fibers, which cause us to itch.

The fact that wounds itch as they're healing is a good sign, as it means our mechanical and chemical systems are properly functioning. It's just bad luck if the healing wound happens to be in the middle of your back, or worse still, under a plaster cast.

⇨ Are Lions Really Afraid of Kitchen Chairs?

The classic image of a lion tamer is a man holding a whip and a wooden kitchen chair while the lion cowers then swipes, unable to get to the man. But you only need to watch one animal documentary about the plains of Africa to realize that a chair is hardly going to be an obstacle for such a powerful cat. Is the formidable lion really afraid?

This style of lion taming was popularized by Clyde Beatty, a famous American animal trainer from the mid-1900s, although he claimed that it was in use when he started in the business.

Beatty believed that it wasn't that the lions were afraid of the chair; it's just that it confused them. In thousands of years of evolutionary development, nothing like the shape of a chair would ever have been encountered by a lion, so they have no built-in mechanism or experience to deal with it. And like all cats, lions are single-minded, and the four legs of the chair waving in the lion's face are enough to make the lion lose focus and get confused. So even if the lion were planning to kill the tamer, the chair would make it lose its train of thought and get distracted.

Adding to the mystique of the kitchen chair, lions are hierarchical, and the tamer spends a lot of time in the lion's cage, chair in hand, training the lion and demonstrating that the man is in charge.

Mind you, while the chair is effective in making the lion back down and be submissive, if the tamer makes a sudden move and pushes the chair too deep into the lion's personal space, then the lion will be inclined to defend itself and attack. It is then that a tamer will quickly realize that a flimsy four-legged wooden kitchen chair is no match at all for the King of the Jungle.

⇨ Is There Really a Calm Before the Storm?

Sometimes at the end of a hot and humid afternoon, everything will suddenly go quiet. The air becomes still, and even the birds stop singing. This is the calm before the storm. A few minutes later the air changes again, the clouds darken and lower, and the storm hits. Why does this happen?

Most storms need warm, moist air for fuel. This air is drawn up to the clouds from the surrounding environment as the storm system develops, leaving a low-pressure vacuum close to the ground. The air travels up through and over the clouds before it descends back down to lower altitudes, pulled by the vacuum that remains. On the way back down, the air becomes warmer and drier. When that warm, stable

air spreads across an area, it makes the rest of the air stable. That is the calm before the storm.

This process does not always happen, and there are many different types of storms. Some don't produce a calming influence at all, and instead are preceded by powerful winds and thunder.

⇨ How Do Arson Investigators Find the Cause of a Fire?

A house or building is completely burnt to the ground and there is nothing left except ashes and smoke. Was it an accident? Was it arson? How can the investigators possibly tell? Here's how.

Because fire consumes evidence, arson is regarded as one of the hardest crimes to identify and verify. It takes years of experience to become an arson investigator, a person who sifts through the debris to find the cause of the fire.

The first thing an investigator does is find the fire's place of origin. If they find the origin, they then have a better chance of determining the cause of the fire. While the "area of origin" can be a larger area such as an entire room, the "point of origin" is the smallest area that can be identified. For example, in the case of a wildland fire, the area of origin might be the size of an acre, while the point of origin could be the size of a campfire. In a house, the area might be a room, while the point might be an electrical outlet.

Once the point of origin is found, the investigator must determine the cause of the fire. This is the hard part. The first thing is to eliminate as many accidental causes as possible, such as faulty appliances, sparks from fireplaces, unattended cigarettes, and faulty wiring.

Once the main accidental possibilities have been ruled out, the ignition source needs to be found to see if the fire was caused by arson. Multiple ignition sites indicate that a fire was intentionally set. Charring on the walls in "V" patterns is a sign of this. The remnants of any combustible materials that may have been used to start the fire also indicate arson, as do chemical accelerants. The investigators use their sense of smell to detect any chemical solvents or alcohol that may have been used to propel the fire. They also use specially trained dogs to assist in this aspect. The dogs are not only able to smell minute amounts of liquid accelerants at the site, but they are also able to smell any that might have been spilled on the clothes of onlookers from the street.

So, while many arsonists might think their fire will destroy all the evidence, the techniques used by arson investigators are remarkably accurate in uncovering the truth.

⇨ Does Warm Water Freeze More Quickly Than Cold Water?

As counterintuitive as it seems, if you've ever tested it, you'll know that warm water freezes faster than cold water. This was first observed by Aristotle in the 4th century BC, and in 1963 became known as the Mpemba effect. Erasto Mpemba was a 13-year-old Tanzanian student who noticed that a hot ice cream mixture froze faster than a cold one. Mpemba later teamed up with a physics professor, and in 1969, published a paper on his findings. The Mpemba effect is definitely known to occur, although a definitive explanation has never been provided. Scientists have offered a number of possibilities.

The most common theory is that warm water evaporates more quickly, making it lose mass. This means it has to lose less heat in order to freeze.

The density of warm water also helps. Molecules in water are bound together by relatively weak forces generated by hydrogen bonds. When these water molecules are warm, the hydrogen bonds stretch and the molecules move farther apart, making the water less dense. This stretching allows the bonds within the water molecules to relax, causing them to give up energy. Giving up energy is the same as cooling, which makes warm water freeze faster than cold water.

Another theory is that water develops convection currents, which are movements within the water, and temperature gradients as it cools. Warm water will have large temperature differences throughout and lose heat more quickly from the surface. Cold water, on the other hand, has less convection and movement to accelerate the freezing process.

Last, there's the science behind how things freeze. Frost has insulating effects, and cold water will tend to freeze at the top first, insulating the rest of the water and reducing further heat loss via radiation and convection. Warm water freezes from the bottom and sides because of the convection currents, meaning it can freeze more uniformly and at a greater speed.

Despite all these detailed theories, the answer may be as simple as this—the heat from the container holding the warm water melts through the layer of frost on the base of the freezer. Without the frost to act as insulation, the container rests on a much colder surface, allowing the water to freeze faster.

⇨ What Is the Meaning of Life?

What is the meaning of life? This one perennial question has perplexed the human race for millennia. It is a very complex question, and the constant search for the answer has produced much theological, psychological, scientific, philosophical, metaphysical, and ideological debate. There is any number of potential answers, depending on which discipline is considered. All of them are highly subjective, but some of the suggestions offered over history are:

- To achieve biological perfection; to live and survive; to adapt and evolve; to reproduce.
- To seek wisdom; to learn lessons from life; to seek knowledge.
- To realize one's potential; to live one's dreams; to make a difference.
- To do good; to be generous and benefit others; to forgive; to be honorable; to leave the world a better place.
- To worship God and enter Heaven; to love God and all his creations; to attain union with God.
- To love and enjoy life; to be compassionate; to seek pleasure and avoid pain.
- To have power; to master the world; to strive for superiority.

- To ensure that life on earth always continues to exist.
- To not seek the meaning of life, because the answer is too profound to be understood. The meaning of life is to forget about the search for the meaning of life, as you will never live if you are looking for this answer.
- Life has no meaning; human existence has no purpose because it occurred out of a random chance of nature.

Will a definitive answer to this age-old question ever be found? Probably not, because there are many answers.

PHOTO CREDITS

All photos from shutterstock.com

page 1: © Chaipanya
page 3: © Ralf Gosch
page 6: © Worrachet Sansing
page 8: © Brent Hofacker
page 10: © Santyaga
page 12: © Quang Ho
page 15: © Anest
page 17: © Muratart
page 18: © Givaga
page 21: © Ezume Images
page 24: © Photographee.eu
page 26: © Tim Ur
page 28: © Kunertus
page 31: © Vladimir Mijailovic
page 33: © Wavebreakmedia
page 35: © Denizo71
page 36: © DJ Taylor
page 38: © Vvoe
page 41: © Hintau Aliaksei
page 43: © Matej Kastelic
page 45: © Mari Swanepoel
page 46: © Robert J. Gatto
page 49: © Poznyakov
page 51: © Matej Kastelic
page 53: © Lyudmila Voronova
page 54: © Vlasov Yevhenii
page 57: © Shane Gross
page 58: © Wisanu Nuu
page 61: © Jacob Lund
page 63: © Casimiro pt
page 65: © Africa Studio
page 67: © Sasa Prudkov
page 69: © Photomediagroup

page 70: © tdee photo cm
page 73: © tortoise: © Michael
   Smith ITWP; turtle: © Fotos593
page 74: © Billion photo
page 77: © Sebra
page 79: © Jurik Peter
page 80: © Mikael Gamkier
page 83: © Vectorfusionart
page 85: © Molnar Photo
page 86: © Daniel Prudek
page 88: © ckp1001
page 90: © Ilya Adnriyanov
page 92: © Gary Yim
page 94: © Lifetimestock
page 96: © Valeria Cantone
page 99: © Denk Creative
page 101: © Sakhorn
page 102: © Cathleen A Clapper
page 105: © Kateryna Larina
page 106: © Hayk Shalunts
page 108: © Wiratchai
   Wansamngam
page 111: © Connors Bros
page 112: © Jabiru
page 115: © saap585
page 116: © Egyptian Studio
page 119: © Todd Castor
page 120: © Iacamerachiara
page 123: © Adwo
page 125: © Vladimir Gjorgiev
page 127: © Miguel Ramirez
page 129: © Eoger Clark Arps
page 131: © Johan Swanepoel

page 132: © Elena Schweitzer

page 135: © Iulian Dragomir

page 137: © Caleb Foster

page 138: © Anetlanda

page 141: © wentus

page 143: © Anneka

page 144: © Pavel1964

page 146: © Fer Gregory

page 148: © Imnoom

page 151: © Hundley Photography

page 152: © Gundam Ai

page 154: © Blueorange Studio

page 157: © KucherAV

page 158: © Mezzotint

page 160: © Agrofruti

page 162: © Ikhyon Kwon

page 164: © Blakeley

page 167: © Reflextions

page 168: © Jim Barber

page 171: © Africa Studio

page 172: © Ruslan Guzov

page 175: © Aspen Photo

page 176: © Torwaistudio

page 178: © Angel Dibilio

page 180: © Marylooo

page 182: © Grandpa

page 184: © Urbanimages

page 187: © Dusan Zidar

page 188: © Henryk Sadura

page 191: © Dewitt

page 193: © Photohraphee.eu

page 195: © Tawin Mukdharakosa

page 196: © i6k

page 199: © Monika Wisniewska

page 201: © Andrey Popov

page 203: © Igor Wheeler

page 205: © Zacarias Pereira da Mata

page 208: © Arena Creative

ABOUT THE AUTHOR

Andrew Thompson divides his time between Australia and England. A lawyer by trade, his obsession with finding out the truth about aspects of the world that we take for granted has led him to accumulate a vast body of knowledge, which he has distilled into book form.

He is the author of the three Ulysses Press best sellers: *What Did We Use Before Toilet Paper?*, *Can Holding in a Fart Kill You?*, and *Hair of the Dog to Paint the Town Red*. See all of Andrew's books at www.andrewthompsonwriter.co.uk or at Twitter @AndrewTWriter.